The EVERYTHING KIDS' ®

Joke Book

Side-splitting, rib-tickling fun!

Michael Dahl

P9-DBY-552

Adams Media Corporation
Holbrook, Massachusetts

An Everything® Series Book.
Everything® is a registered trademark of Adams Media Corporation.

Published by Adams Media Corporation
260 Center Street, Holbrook, MA 02343
www.adamsmedia.com

ISBN: 1-58062-495-2

Printed in the United States of America.

J I H G F E D C B A

Library of Congress Cataloging-in-Publication Data
Dahl, Michael.
    The everything kids' joke book / Michael Dahl.
        p. cm.
    ISBN 1-58062-495-2
    1. Wit and humor, Juvenile. [1. Jokes. 2. Riddles.] I. Title.
PN6163.D34 2001
    818'.602—dc21   2001022047

This publication is designed to provide accurate and authoritative information with regard to the subject
matter covered. It is sold with the understanding that the publisher is not engaged in rendering legal,
accounting, or other professional advice. If legal advice or other expert assistance is required, the services
of a competent professional person should be sought.
                                        — From a *Declaration of Principles* jointly adopted
                                          by a Committee of the American Bar Association
                                          and a Committee of Publishers and Associations

Cover illustrations by Joseph Sherman.
Interior illustrations by Kurt Dolber.
Puzzles by Beth Blair.
Series editor: Cheryl Kimball

Puzzle Power Software by Centron Software Technologies, Inc. was used to create puzzle grids.

This book is available at quantity discounts for bulk purchases.
For information, call 1-800-872-5627.

See the entire Everything® series at *everything.com*.

Dedication

To Danny Thomas for laughing in all the right places

Acknowledgments

Just as Dante had his famous Three Ladies who guided him through his *Divine Comedy*, I had three marvelous women who escorted me through my considerably more down-to-earth comical venture: Kathleen Baxter who pointed the way, Jeanne Hanson who opened the door, and Cheryl Kimball who polished everything up nice and shiny. Grazie, ladies.

Hats off to my witty friends and family who shared a few of their favorite jokes, gags, and silly stories: Gene and Shirley Dahl, Gerry Thomas, Matthew and Alex Rooney, Kyle and Nathaniel Thomas, Thom Melcher, Kurt Larson, Kevin McLaughlin, Jon Mikkelsen, and Jimmy Fairburn.

Contents

Introduction

Humans are the only creatures on this planet who laugh. Oh sure, hyenas make a funny bark that may sound like a laugh. Grade B movies and sitcoms show chimpanzees and dolphins laughing at their silly human costars. But people are the only animals that giggle, chuckle, titter, guffaw, belly laugh, chortle, and yuck. Have you ever known a hamster who snickers at an elephant joke? Or a Rottweiler who appreciates a well-thrown custard pie in his face? Didn't think so.

Besides loving to laugh, we also like making other people laugh. Who hasn't enjoyed being the center of attention, even if only for a few seconds, after you've told a truly terrific joke? Well, this book has tons of them—jokes, howlers, groaners, puns, witty retorts, and practical gags. It also has advice on how to tell a joke, how to create your own jokes, how to do standup comedy, and reveals inside information (and secrets) of the world's greatest comedians.

One more thing. This book is not to be read in the silence of your bedroom or favorite hiding place. Carry it with you at all times, read it out loud, underline the best parts, dog-ear the pages, share the jokes with all your friends.

Read, laugh, and be more funny!

Jokes, Gags, Puns, and More!

Monster Mania

What kind of dog does Dracula have as a pet?
A bloodhound.

What is the Mummy's favorite music?
Wrap.

Why did King Kong climb to the top of the
Empire State Building?
He was too big to use the elevator.

What sport do vampires like to watch?
Bat-minton.

Why are most mummies vain and conceited?
They're all wrapped up in themselves.

Why did the dragon cough during the day?
Because he smoked knights.

Why is Frankenstein such a good gardener?
He has a green thumb.

Did you hear about the old vampire who kept
his teeth in the freezer?
He gave his victims frostbite.

The little vampire could never gain weight.
His eating was all in vein.

Why does the mad scientist like to eat a hot
dog with a glass of beer?
It's a frank and stein.

Did you hear about the zombie hairdresser?
Each day she dyed on the job.

Why did the cheerleading squad move into the
haunted house?
Because it's got spirit!

Where does Godzilla sleep?
Anywhere he wants to!

What do you get when you cross a ghost with a firecracker?
Bamboo!

Did you hear about the two vampires who raced one another?
It was neck and neck.

Why are cannibals so popular?
I don't know, but they always have lots of friends for lunch!

What did one casket say to the other casket?
"Is that you coffin?"

Hole In One

Fill in the missing letters in the words below. Then, copy the letter from each word into the box with the same number. When you're finished, you'll get the answer to this riddle: What did the witch use to fix her broken jack-o'-lantern? HINT: Be careful! Sometimes more than one letter can finish a word. Be sure each letter makes sense in the final answer.

What did the witch use to fix her broken jack-o'-lantern?

1. __UPPY
2. J__MP
3. LU__P
4. HAP__Y
5. SHAR__
6. SM__LE
7. SA__D
8. SLOP__Y
9. S__D
10. __UNA
11. __HURCH
12. C__INA

She used a

1	2	3	4	5	6	7
8	9	10	11	12		

3

What's Dracula's least favorite food?
A steak. It goes right through him and leaves a nasty case of heartburn.

How many dead people are in the graveyard?
All of them!

Sickos

What do beekeepers get?
Hives.

What do airline pilots get?
Flu.

What do computer geeks get?
Slipped discs.

If athletes get athlete's foot, what do astronauts get?
Missile toe.

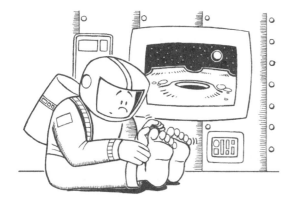

What do firefighters get?
Water on the knee.

What do workers at McDonald's get?
Fallen arches.

What do carpenters get?
Hangnail.

What do roofers get?
Shingles.

What do spies get?
See-sickness.

What do basketball players get?
Hooping cough.

What do watchmakers get?
All wound up!

What's Gnu?

Mona: I had trouble with my horse yesterday. I wanted to go in one direction, and he wanted to go in another.
Sam: So how did you decide?
Mona: He tossed me for it.

Sam: I think my pet duck is broken.
Mona: Broken?
Sam: Yeah, he has a quack in him.

JOKIN' AROUND

Fowl Definitions
From the Dictionary for Bird-Brains

Hatchet—What a chicken does with its eggs.

Information—How geese fly.

Foul ball—An egg.

Crow bar—Where birds like to drink and hang out.

Mona: What's worse than a giraffe with a sore throat?
Sam: A centipede with athlete's foot.

Sam: I'd like to buy a bird.
Store Clerk: How about a talking mynah?
Sam: Sounds great!
Store Clerk: This one here is very talented. She can talk in seven languages, sing *The Star-Spangled Banner*, and recite the Gettysburg Address.
Sam: Never mind that. Is she tender?

Rich Snob: I don't like your bird, young man.
Sam: Why not?
Rich Snob: Because every time I walk by, it says, "Cheap! Cheap!"

Why did the hen slide her eggs down the hill?
She loved playing with the children.

How much fur can you get from a skunk?
As fur as you possibly can!

How do you spell mousetrap with only three letters?
C-A-T

Mona: What kind of pet can you stand on?
Sam: A car-pet.

Mona: What kind of pet makes the loudest noise?
Sam: A trum-pet.

Mona: What kind of pet can help you write letters?
Sam: The alpha-pet.

Alex: Why is that dachshund sitting in the sun?
Amy: Because his owners like hot dogs.

Do you know how to raise rabbits?
Yes, by the scruff of their necks.

Sam: Wow! It's raining cats and dogs.
Mona: How can you tell?
Sam: I just stepped in a poodle.

Sam: Have you ever seen a fish bowl?
Mona: Sure, lots of times.
Sam: How do they get their fins into those little holes?

Mona:
Do you sell alligator shoes?
Store Clerk: Yes, we do.
What size does your alligator wear?

Father Kangaroo: Why are you scratching?
Mother Kangaroo: The kids are eating crackers in bed again.

Sam: Can you name four members of the cat family?
Mona: Papa Cat, Mama Cat, and two kittens.

Mona: How did the pig write his name?
Sam: He used an *oink*-pen.

What did the leopard say after dinner?
"That hit just the right spots."

Sam: Hey! Your dog bit my ankle.
Mona: Sorry, but that's as high as he can reach.

Mona: How do you keep a wild elephant from charging?
Sam: Take away his credit card.

Why Oh Why?

Pick up words as the chicken walks from START to END. Write each word down in the order in which the chicken finds them, and you'll end up with the answer to this riddle:

Why did the chicken cross the playground?

1	2	3	4	5	6

Write the answer here.

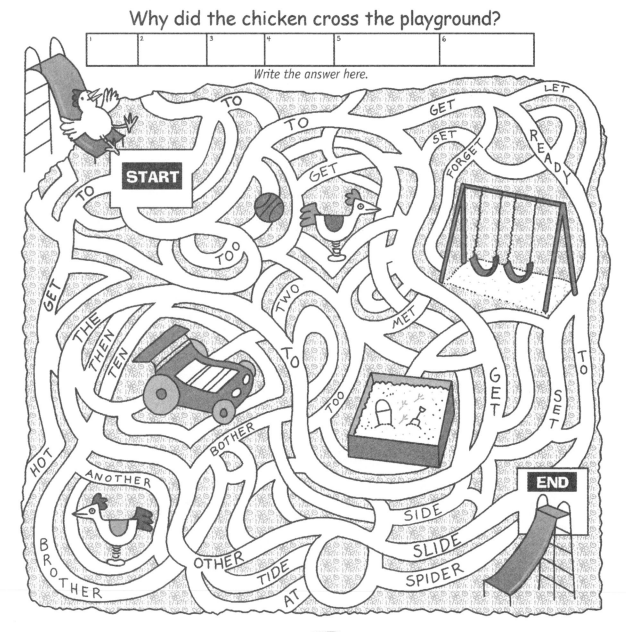

7

Why does a flamingo stand up on one leg?
Because if he pulled the other one up he'd fall over.

Mona: My pony sounds funny.
Sam: That's because he's a little hoarse.

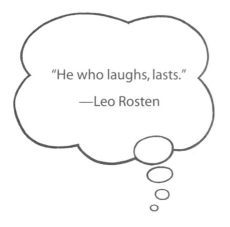

"He who laughs, lasts."
—Leo Rosten

Mona: Why do hummingbirds hum?
Sam: They don't know the words.

What did the little kid say when he saw the peacock?
"Look, Ma, the chicken's in bloom!"

Sam: I haven't seen your pet chicken lately.
Mona: Well, this week she's been laying low.

WORDS to KNOW

Punch line: the part of the joke that gets the laugh

The animal doctor is always busy as a bee!
Take a gander at a few of his patients:

The leopard is seeing spots,
The kangaroo is feeling jumpy,
The goldfish is flushed,
The chameleon is looking green,
The woodpecker caught a bug,
*The baby duckling has been getting a little
    down lately,*
And the bullfrog is afraid he's going to croak!

Crazy Colors (or Hue Must Be Nuts!)

What color is a marriage?
Wed.

What color is an echo?
YELL-oohhhhhhh!

What color is a ghost?
Boo.

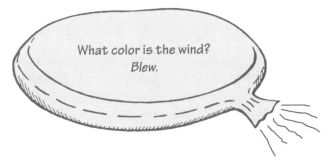

What color is the wind?
Blew.

What color is a baby ghost?
Baby boo.

What color is a kitten's meow?
Purr-ple.

What color is a soccer score?
Goaled!

What color is a police investigation?
Copper.

What color is a witch's potion?
Bracken brew.

Computer Wonks

Why did the computer geek sell his cat?
He was afraid it would eat his mouse.

How do you contact Hercules by computer?
Send him he-mail.

What has a video screen, a keyboard, six legs, and plugs into the wall?
A computer bug.

What do computer geeks eat for dessert?
Apple pie a la modem.

Did you hear about the geek who almost drowned?
He was surfing the Web and got bumped off.

JOKIN' AROUND

Totally Buggy

Computer Viruses to Watch Out For:

The Disney Virus
The screen starts acting Goofy.

The Titanic Virus
Everything goes down.

The Diet Virus
The computer quits after just one byte.

The Las Vegas Virus
Users have to turn in their chips.

The Divorce Virus
Your motherboard stops
talking to your data.

Nerd: Why is my computer screen all wet?
Dweeb: I was trying to send e-mail, but the
stamps kept sliding off!

Did you hear about the guy who flunked
technical college?
He can only operate nincomputers.

Nerd: How many bytes are in your software
program?
Dweeb: I'll let you know as soon as I've
finished eating it.

Mother: Having trouble with your computer, son?
Karl: My PC says it can't see my printer.
Mother: I'm not surprised. Look how messy
your room is!

Nerd: Do you have a cursor on your computer?
Dweeb: I'll say! You should just hear the words
my dad uses when the computer goes
down!

Nerd: What's wrong with your keyboard?
Dweeb: Myspacebarseemstobestuck.

You heard about the computer scientist who
spends half his time directing the town's
orchestra?
He's a semi-conductor.

"Of course I know how to copy disks . . .
Where's the Xerox machine?"

If at first you don't succeed . . . call it version 1.0.

What was the world's first computer?
An Apple. Eve gave one to Adam.

What are the three main parts of a printer?
The power cord, the jammed paper tray, and the blinking light.

"My computer is almost human."
"What do you mean?"
"When it makes a mistake, it blames it on another computer."

I had a rotten day at work today. My computer broke down and I had to think all day long.

Tom and Tina Swifties

"Look at the cute pony," said Tina a little hoarsely.

"I can't remember what groceries I need," said Tom listlessly.

"Is it time to turn the pancakes?" asked Tina flippantly.

"Look at that scroungy old dog," Tom muttered.

"Who cut the cheese?" asked Tina sharply.

"I'd gladly give you a thousand dollars," said Tom grandly.

"My pet bird is sick," said Tina illegally.

"Let's set up camp," said Tom intently.

"I'll make the fire," Tina bellowed.

"I got the lowest grade in my cooking class," said Tom degradedly.

"We're all out of pumpernickel bread," said Tina wryly.

"Why can't we go bowling?" Tom bawled.

"I finished taking my shower," said Tina dryly.

"Give me another strawberry cake," Tom retorted.

"These oysters are all mine!" said Tina shellfishly.

"Keep them! I prefer other seafood," said Tom crabbily.

"I love arithmetic," Tina added.

"And I love correcting my mistakes," Tom remarked.

"That's my gold mine," Tina claimed.

"But it used to be mine!" Tom exclaimed.

Didja Hear?

Didja hear about the police officer who arrested the young cat?
He saw the kitty litter.

Didja hear about the baby girl who wanted to play basketball?
She had trouble dribbling.

Didja hear about the taxicab driver who lost his job?
He was driving away all his customers.

Didja hear about the pet shop owner who couldn't get sell his porcupine?
He was stuck with it.

Didja hear about the cannibal who ate his mother's sister?
He was an aunt-eater.

Didja hear about the woman who'd buy anything that was marked down?
She came home with an elevator.

Didja hear about the sailor who was kicked off the submarine?
He liked sleeping with the windows open.

Picto-Laugh #1

A pictograph is a very simple drawing of something funny. Can you guess what this little picto-laugh is showing? HINT: Think about something itsy-bitsy!

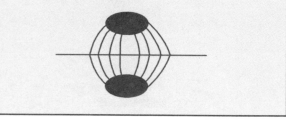

Say What?

Figure out where to put each of the scrambled letters. They all fit in spaces under their own columns. When you fill in the grid, you will have the answer to the following riddle: Didja hear about the piano tuner who was arrested at the aquarium?

Didja hear about
the piano tuner
who was arrested
at the aquarium?

Didja hear about the rubber man from the circus who was killed in an auto wreck?
He died in his own arms.

Didja hear about the lady who stopped feeding the pigeons?
The birds revolted and formed a coo.

Didja hear about the magician who was walking down the street and turned into a drugstore?

Didja hear about the kitten that loves to play with a piece of string?
After a while he has a ball.

Larry and Luna

Luna: My poor cat doesn't have a nose!
Larry: How does she smell?
Luna: Terrible!

Luna: I must be sick. I'm seeing spots.
Larry: Have you seen a doctor?
Luna: No, just spots.

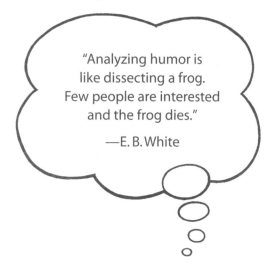

"Analyzing humor is like dissecting a frog. Few people are interested and the frog dies."

—E. B. White

Luna: Why is it better to buy a thermometer in the winter?
Larry: Because in summer they go up!

Luna: My candy bar is missing.
Larry: That's too bad, because it tasted delicious.

Luna: What's the last thing you take off before you go to bed?
Larry: My feet off the floor.

Larry: How many feet are in a yard?
Luna: That depends on how many people are standing in it.

Luna: How many seconds are in a year?
Larry: Twelve.
Luna: Only twelve! Are you sure?
Larry: Yeah, the second of January, the second of February . . .

Luna: I can tell the future.
Larry: Really?
Luna: Yes. I can tell you what the score of a soccer game is before it even starts.
Larry: What is it?
Luna: Nothing to nothing.

Larry: What's the best thing to put in a pie?
Luna: Your teeth!

Luna: Do you know how long the world's longest nose was?
Larry: Eleven inches.
Luna: That's not very long.
Larry: If it was any longer it would be a foot.

"The most wasted of all days is one without laughter."

—e.e. cummings

Larry: Did I tell you my mom's been in the hospital for years?
Luna: Wow! She must really be sick.
Larry: Nah, she's a doctor.

Luna: I just got back from the beauty shop.
Larry: It was closed, huh?

Larry: There's something wrong with that pizza I ate.
Luna: How do you know?
Larry: Inside information.

Larry: How do you keep a skunk from smelling?
Luna: Plug his nose!

Luna: Is there any tapioca pudding on the menu?
Waiter: There was, but I wiped it off.

Larry: Why are you scratching yourself?
Luna: Because I'm the only person who knows where it itches.

Larry: What did you think of the Grand Canyon?
Luna: It was just gorges!

Luna: Who was that on the phone?
Larry: Some joker. He said, "It's long-distance from Japan," and I said, "It sure is!" and hung up.

Larry: Boy! My diet must be working.
Luna: Why do you say that?
Larry: I can finally see the numbers on the bathroom scale.

Larry: I'm on a new diet. I only eat food that swims.
Luna: That sounds great! Fish is very healthy for you.
Larry: Yuck, forget fish! Do you realize how much trouble I'm having teaching a cow to dog-paddle?

Larry: Do you believe in astrology?
Luna: No, it's just a lot of Taurus.

School Jokes

Alex: Teacher! Teacher! Jimmy just swallowed four quarters!
Teacher: Now, why would he do that?
Alex: It's his lunch money.

Alex: Teacher! Teacher! Now, Jimmy swallowed all his pennies. And it's your fault!
Teacher: Why is it my fault?
Alex: You told him he needed more sense.

Teacher: You need to study harder, Alex. Why, when I was your age, I could recite all the presidents' names by heart.
Amy: Yeah, but there were only two or three back then.

Teacher: Where are all the kings and queens of England crowned?
Amy: On the tops of their heads.

Teacher: Give me a sentence using the word "gladiator."
Alex: The lion ate my bossy Aunt Mimi, and I'm glad he ate her!

Teacher: Correct this sentence: "Aliens is in the classroom."
Alex: Forget the sentence, Teach! Run for your life!

Teacher: Tell me how you'd use the word "rhythm" in a sentence.
Alex: My older brother is going to the movies, and I want to go rhythm.

Teacher: Where can you find the Red Sea?
Amy: Usually on my report card.

Teacher: Let's do a simple math lesson. How many fingers do you have?
Alex: Ten.
Teacher: And if three fingers were taken away, what would you have?
Alex: I would have to give up my saxophone lessons!

Boggle Box

In his bestselling book, *The BFG* (Big Friendly Giant), author Roald Dahl's giant hero has his own name for everything. For instance, a school is called a "boggle box." If you've ever been to school—and who hasn't?—you'll know that the name fits!

Teacher: Name a creature that is very good at catching flies.
Amy: A baseball player in left field.

Teacher: Can you use the word "fascinate" in a sentence?
Alex: Yeah. My jacket has ten buttons, but I can only fasten eight.

Teacher: Can anyone tell me what a myth is?
Amy: A female moth.

Mother: Explain this "D" on your test, dear.
Amy: I'm having trouble with my Is.
Mother: You need new glasses?
Amy: No, I can't spell "Mississippi"!

Teacher: Did you wake up grouchy this morning, young man?
Alex: No, Dad and I let her sleep.

Teacher: Who was Joan of Arc?
Alex: Noah's wife.

Alex: Why are kindergarten teachers so optimistic?
Amy: Cuz every day they try to make the little things count.

Teacher: How did you get so messy?
Amy: I had an inkling of what I wanted to write my report about. So I grabbed a pen and paper.
Teacher: And then?
Amy: Then my pen had an inkling all over my shirt!

Teacher: Tell me the name of the Prince of Wales.
Amy: Orca.

Mother: I don't think my child deserves a zero on this test.
Teacher: Neither do I, ma'am. But it's the lowest score I can give!

Teacher: Use the word "paradox" in a sentence.
Alex: The hunter shot a paradox flying over the lake.

Mother: Your teacher tells me you're at the bottom of the class.
Angie: Yeah, but they teach the same thing at both ends.

Teacher: Why were you late to school?
Amy: There are eight in my family, Teach, but the clock was only set for seven.

Mother: Why don't you like your new teacher, honey?
Amy: Because she told me to sit in the front row for the present. And then she never gave me any present!

Mother: Why did you have to stay after school today, Alex?
Alex: I flunked the test. I didn't know where the Appalachians were.
Mother: Well, next time remember where you put things, dear.

Teacher: That makes five times I've had to punish you this week, Darren. What do you have to say for yourself?
Darren: I'm glad it's Friday!

Alex: Would you yell at me for something I didn't do? *Teacher:* Certainly not. *Alex:* Good, because I didn't do my homework.

Quickies

One microbe ran into another microbe while swimming through a bloodstream.

"You don't look so hot," said the first microbe.

"I feel terrible," said the second microbe. "I think I'm coming down with penicillin."

If we breathe oxygen during the day, what do we breath at night?
Nitrogen.

"I think the cuckoo in my cuckoo clock is tired."
"That's silly!"
"No, it's not. You'd be tired too if you'd been running all night."

What's the hardest thing about falling out of bed?
The floor.

Sounds Funny To Me

Match each funny sound riddle to the correct picture punchline.

1. What goes "Z-Z-U-B, Z-Z-U-B, Z-Z-U-B"?
2. What goes "HOE, HOE, HOE"?
3. What goes "ABCDEFGHIJKLMNOPQRSTUVWXYZ— sluuuuurp"?

4. What goes "HA, HA, HA—thump"?
5. What goes "99 thump, 99 thump, 99 thump"?
6. What goes "tick-WOOF, tick-WOOF, tick-WOOF"?

What did the princess say while she waited for her photos to come back from the store?
"Some day my prints will come!"

Terry: Why is the Mississippi River so rich?
Nick: Because it has two banks and it makes deposits all day long.

Why are you taking that hammer to bed?
So I can get up at the crack of dawn!

What do you get for the man who has everything?
A burglar alarm!

"Long distance? I'd like to place a call to Aberystwyth, Wales."
"Could you spell that please?"
"If I could spell it, I'd write!"

How do robots celebrate Mother's Day?
They send a dozen red roses to the power company.

Judge: This is the last time I want to see you in my court! Do you realize that for the last twenty years, I've seen you in here at least once a month?
Crook: Sorry, your Honor. But it's not my fault that you haven't been promoted.

Karl: Boy, am I mad at my brother!
Trent: What did he do?
Karl: I let him ride my new bicycle, and I told him to treat it as if it were his own.
Trent: So?
Karl: He sold it.

Molar: Hey, why are you getting all dressed up?
Wisdom Tooth: The dentist is taking me out tonight.

"You're very healthy," said the doctor. "You should live to be eighty."
"But, I am eighty!" said the patient.
"See? What did I tell you?"

A young fellow was walking through an unfamiliar part of town late at night. Two muggers jumped out from the shadows and dragged him to the ground. The young guy put up quite a fight, but eventually the two thugs overpowered him.

One of the muggers grabbed the man's wallet, looked inside, and then threw it down in disgust.

"You put up all that fight for just a measly two bucks?" said the mugger.

The fellow answered, "Shucks, no. I was afraid you were gonna find the three hundred dollars I hide in my shoe."

What's the hottest day of the week?
Fry day.

What's the unhappiest day of the week?
Sadder day.

What's the driest day of the week?
Thirst day.

"Could you fix the volume on my car horn?"
"Is it broken?"
"No, but my brakes are."

Darren: Every time I have a cup of coffee, I get a sharp pain in my right eye. What should I do, Doctor?
Doctor: Take the spoon of out your cup.

Mother: Jenny, have you finished filling up the salt shakers yet?

Jenny: No, Mom. It's hard pushing the salt through those tiny holes.

Trent: Is there a place where I can catch the 1:30 bus to town?

Danny: That depends on how fast you can run. It left ten minutes ago.

A father saw his son out in the backyard cleaning their homemade swing, a rubber tire hanging by a rope from a tree branch. The son was hosing it down, wiping it off, dusting out the inside. The puzzled father went outside and said, "Son, I thought you were playing on the golf course with your friends this afternoon." "I was," replied the boy. "But the golf instructor said I needed to improve my swing."

Perry: Officer! Somebody stole my car!

Police Officer: Did you see who did it?

Perry: No, but I got the license number.

Two women met at a laundromat. As they talked, the first woman said, "I have five children." The other woman said, "That sounds nice. I wish I had five children." "Don't you have any children?" asked the first woman. "Yeah, ten!" said the second.

JOKIN' AROUND

Eye to Eye

Make this statement to a friend: "I can put this sheet of paper down on the floor, and I'll bet we can both stand on it, but you won't be able to touch me." Your friend will be eager to take such an easy bet.

Lay the sheet of paper down in a doorway. Shut the door carefully so that the two ends of the sheet stick out on either side. *Voila!* You and your friend will be able to stand on the sheet on opposite sides of the door. But neither of you can touch the other person.

Bet won!

Tip: This trick works even better with an extra long sheet of paper.

Outta This World

Why are astronauts always so clean?
Because they take meteor showers.

Which tastes better, a comet or an asteroid?
An asteroid, because it's meteor.

How is a comet like the dog Wishbone?
They're both stars with tails.

What planet goes up in the summer and down in the winter?
Mercury.

Where do astronauts eat?
The lunch-pad.

How do astronauts keep their rockets free from dust?
They drive through the vacuum of outer space.

What is at the center of Jupiter?
The letter "I."

Why couldn't the astronauts land on the moon?
Because it was full.

Why did the cowboy want to buy a satellite?
So he could watch where he was going when it got dark.

Did you hear about the astronomer who got knocked out?
He's seeing stars.

Where can you see new stars?
In Hollywood.

Astronaut: What's the difference between a Martian burp and a sandstorm?
Astronut: Sandstorms don't glow in the dark.

Alien: I was born on the planet Neptune.
Scientist: That's amazing! Which part?
Alien: All of me.

Astronaut: What are you digging in your pockets for?
Astronut: You said we'd be landing this thing at a meteor, and most parking meteors only take quarters.

Did you hear about the young girl who plans to be an astronaut?
Her teacher says she's taking up space!

Did you hear about the Martian who flew to Earth to buy a brand new car for his family? He told the car salesman, "I want the body green, the wheels green, the interior green, and the windows tinted green." The salesman said, "No problem." After the Martian ordered his new car, he made an interplanetary long-distance call to his wife to tell her the good news. "That's terrific, honey," said his wife. "But what color is it?" "Flesh tones," said the Martian.

Did you hear about that new restaurant on the moon? Great food, but no atmosphere.

What's the only Irish constellation?
Orion.

"Sir, do you believe in UFOs?"
"No comet."

Two Venusians landed in front of a busy stoplight.
The first one said, "She's cute. I saw her first."
The second one said, "Yeah, but I'm the one she winked at."

What do astronauts take for a headache?
Space capsules.

"I just got back from the Dog Star."
"Sirius?"

If astronauts are so smart, why do they count backwards?

Scientist: Your mission is to land on the Sun.
Astronaut: Are you nuts? I'll burn up!
Scientist: That's why you're going at night.

Two Martians landed their spacecraft in a quiet stretch of countryside.
   "I think this must be a human cemetery," said the first Martian. "See that marker over there? It's a gravestone. And it gives the human's age, too—one hundred and two."
   "What was his name?" asked the second Martian.
   "Miles to Milwaukee."

Professor Fruitcake

Did you hear about the mad scientist who married the Amish woman?
He drove her buggy.

Did you hear about the mad scientist who worked for the woman peanut farmer?
He made her nuts.

Did you hear about the mad scientist who trained the Olympic diver?
He sent him off the deep end.

Did you hear about the mad scientist who worked with the bungee jumper?
He pushed him over the edge.

Did you hear about the poor little baby who stayed with the mad scientist?
It went ga-ga.

Did you hear about the rocket experts who hired the mad scientist?
They went ballistic.

Hinky-Pinkys

What's a phony serpent?
A fake snake.

What do you call a chubby dog?
A round hound.

What's a big dance in a cemetery?
A grave rave.

What's a purple gorilla?
A grape ape.

What do phantoms eat for breakfast?
Ghost toast.

What's a frightening pet bird?
A scary canary.

What's a glove for a small cat?
A kitten mitten.

What's a happy-go-lucky Thanksgiving bird?
A perky turkey.

What do you call a frog whose car broke down?
A towed toad.

Hink Pink Kriss Kross

The answers to these Hink Pinks are two rhyming words of one syllable each. Fill each answer into the numbered Kriss Kross grid. Surprise—you've got one done!

ACROSS

3 happy boy
4 a fruity drink at noon
6 a cooking vessel that's not cool
8 a counterfeit reptile
10 a musical piece that's not short
11 home of a small rodent
12 large amount of fake hair
13 enjoyable joke that makes you groan

DOWN

1 a sick dollar
2 football players yelling together
3 great group of marching musicians
5 a chilly place to swim
7 skinny female monarch
9 large branch

Who works at a school for monsters?
A creature teacher.

What do you call a tired tent?
A sleepy teepee.

Who's the spooky leader of a church?
A sinister minister.

What's do you call a magician who works with reptiles?
A lizard wizard.

What's a fish who works in the operating room?
A sturgeon surgeon.

25

What do you call your crazy best friend?
A nutty buddy.

What do you call your pet pooch that got caught in the rain?
A soggy doggy.

What do you call a parent with six crying babies?
A diaper wiper!

What do you call Her Royal Highness's denim pants?
The Queen's jeans.

What do you call that dumb little guy who flies around and shoots arrows on Valentine's Day?
Stupid Cupid.

What's reddish yellow and helps a door swing back and forth?
An orange door hinge.

Ring the Doorbell! (Knock Knock Jokes)

Knock knock.
Who's there?
Sarah.
Sarah who?
Sarah a doctor in the house?

Knock knock.
Who's there?
Dwayne.
Dwayne who?
Dwayne the bathtub, I'm dwowning!

Knock knock.
Who's there?
Amos.

Amos who?
A mosquito bit me!

Knock knock.
Who's there?
Annie.
Annie who?
Annie bit me again!

Knock knock.
Who's there?
Wendy.
Wendy who?
Wendy you want to go to the movies?

Knock knock.
Who's there?
Juicy.
Juicy who?
Juicy who threw that snowball at me?

Knock knock.
Who's there?
Phillip.
Phillip who?
Phillip my bag with candy! It's Halloween!

"In the end, everything is a gag."
—Charlie Chaplin

Knock knock.
Who's there?
Arthur.
Arthur who?
Arthur any cookies left?

Knock knock.
Who's there?
Iris.
Iris who?
I received a package in the mail.

Knock knock.
Who's there?
Sharon.
Sharon who?
Sharon share alike.

Knock knock.
Who's there?
Wilfred.
Wilfred who?
Will Fred come out and play today?

Knock knock.
Who's there?
Hugh.
Hugh who?
Yoo-hoo to you, too!

Knock knock.
Who's there?
Rita.
Rita who?
Rita good book lately?

Knock knock.
Who's there?
Boo.
Boo who?
Why are you crying?

Knock knock.
Who's there?
William.
William who?
William make me dinner if I stop knocking?

Knock knock.
Who's there?
Ira.
Ira who?
Ira member you, why don't you remember me?

Knock knock.
Who's there?
Upton.
Upton who?
Upton now it's been pretty quiet around here.

Knock knock.
Who's there?
Olive.
Olive who?
Olive you, do you love me?

Knock knock.
Who's there?
LaToya.
LaToya who?
LaToya store's open, let's go shopping!

Knock knock.
Who's there?
Hutch.
Hutch who?
Gesundheit!

Knock knock.
Who's there?
Dude.
Dude who?
Dude-doo is all over my front yard. Will you please watch your puppy!

Knock knock.
Who's there?
Champ.
Champ who?
Champoo the dog, he's got fleas!

JOKIN' AROUND

Three Blind Mice

Look at the dice below:

Challenge your friends to take three dice, place one on a table or napkin, and balance the other two on top, side by side. First, show them how it's done. Your friends will not be able to reproduce the trick! No matter how hard they try, their top two dice will always fall off the bottom one.

How did you do it?

Spit. (No, not now!) That's the secret of the trick: spit. During the setup of the trick, while no one is paying attention to your hands, lick one of your fingertips. Then touch one of the die faces. A tiny amount of saliva will hold the two dice together, especially if you hold the dice tightly together for a second or two.

Tip: It's important to place the top two dice with the 2 and the 4 showing (as in the illustration). Why? Because then the facing sides become the 1s on each die. The faces with 1s provide more surface area to hold your secret saliva.

When you hand the dice to your opponent, wipe off the tell-tale "glue" without drawing attention. Use your hands to rub off the spit or push the dice across the tablecloth or napkin.

29

Knock knock.
Who's there?
Banana.
Banana who?
Knock knock.
Who's there?
Banana.
Banana who?
Knock knock.
Who's there?
Banana.
Banana who?
Knock knock.
Who's there?
Orange.
Orange who?
Orange you glad I stopped saying banana?

Knock knock.
Who's there?
Edith.
Edith who?
Edith thick joothy hamburger for thupper.

Knock knock.
Who's there?
Tank.
Tank who?
You're very welcome.

Knock knock.
Who's there?
Toodle.
Toodle who?
Ta-ta!

Knock knock.
Who's there?
Hope.
Hope who?
Hopen the door and let me in!

Knock knock.
Who's there?
Donnelly.
Donnelly who?
Donnelly've me out here in the dark!

Knock knock.
Who's there?
A little old lady.
A little old lady who?
I didn't know you could yodel.

Knock knock.
Who's there?
Chester.
Chester who?
Chester little kid.

Knock knock.
Who's there?
Aubrey.
Aubrey who?
Aubrey quiet!

Knock knock.
Who's there?
Skid.
Skid who?
Forget it! I'm staying right here.

Knock knock.
Who's there?
Juan.
Juan who?
Juan to buy some candy for the school band?

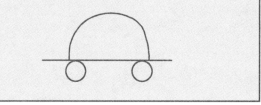

Picto-Laugh #2

A pictograph is a very simple drawing of something funny. Can you guess what this little picto-laugh is showing? HINT: Think about something slow on something fast!

Knock knock.
Who's there?
Theophilus.
Theophilus who?
The awfullest storm I've ever seen out here!

Knock knock.
Who's there?
Ash.
Ash who?
Ash sure could use some help out in the garden.

Knock knock.
Who's there?
Alex.
Alex who?
Alex some more soda pop, please.

Knock knock.
Who's there?
Pete.
Pete who?
Pizza's here!

Knock knock.
Who's there?
Giovanni.
Giovanni who?
Giovanni extra topping on that?

Knock knock.
Who's there?
Wanda.
Wanda who?
Wanda be a millionaire?

Knock knock.
Who's there?
Yah.
Yah who?
I didn't know you were a cowboy.

Knock knock.
Who's there?
Matthew.
Matthew who.
Matthew a thilly queth-tion?

Knock knock.
Who's there?
Isabelle.
Isabelle who?
Isabelle working, or should I just keep knocking?

Knock knock.
Who's there?
Oswald.
Oswald who?
Oswald my bubble gum!

Knock knock.
Who's there?
Howard.
Howard who?
Howard you like to step outside?

Knock knock.
Who's there?
Howie.
Howie who?
I'm fine, thanks, how are you?

Knock knock.
Who's there?
Ivan.
Ivan who?
Ivan idea you know who this is.

Knock knock.
Who's there?
Tasha.
Tasha who?
Tasha soccer ball out and let's play!

Knock knock.
Who's there?
Dewey. Dewey who?
Dewey have to listen to any more knock knock jokes?

Jurassic Pork

Why are the dinosaurs extinct?
They smelled so bad.

What do you say when you want your dinosaur to move faster?
"Pronto, saurus!"

Why don't you ever let a tyrannosaur drive your car?
Because a tyrannosaurus rex.

Why are meteors better than toilet paper?
Because one meteor was able to wipe out all the dinosaurs in the world.

Why did the caveman always show up at the party first?
He was Early Man.

What do you call the first man who discovered fire?
Toast.

What did the cavewoman say when she found bugs crawling under a rock?
"Dinner's ready!"

What do you call the remains of a woolly mammoth?
A fuzzle.

What do you call a dinosaur stuck in a glacier?
A fossicle.

What do you get when you cross a dinosaur with a pig?
Jurassic Pork.

Why did the dinosaur cross the road?
Chickens hadn't evolved yet.

Knock knock.
Who's there?
Iguanodon.
Iguanodon who?
Iguanodon town to see the dinosaur exhibit.

Then there was the caveboy who invented the wheel. He told his buddies to keep it a secret. "Don't tell my dad," he said. "Or he'll make me invent the garage."

What do pterodactyls have that no other creature has?
Little pterodactyls.

What toys did cavekids play with?
Tricera-tops.

A full grown stegosaurus can grow up to how many feet?
Just the four.

The world's first glacier was spotted by a caveman with good ice sight.

Cavepeople invented the world's first music by rolling boulders down a hill. They called it rock-and-roll.

Teacher: Why were there no humans alive during the dinosaur age?
Alex: Because it was Pre-Stork times.

JOKIN' AROUND

Double or Nothing

Tell a friend or an adult that you will be able to double their money without buying anything, going on the Stock Exchange, or using a computer. Then ask them for a dollar bill.

Simply fold the bill in half and say, "There! I doubled your money!"

Did you hear about the cavewoman who found a saber-toothed tiger trapped in a block of ice? She quickly built a fire and melted the ice, releasing the dangerous creature. After the tiger carried off her husband, her neighbors asked her why she had done it. "I made a terrible mistake," she said. "I thought I thawed a pussycat!"

Gross!

A man is racing to the bathroom, a second man is leaving it, and a third man is still inside. Can you guess their nationalities?
Russian, Finnish, and European.

What did Mother say to Father when their baby boy fell down the stairs?
"Oh, look, honey! Our little boy is taking his first twenty-three steps!"

Mother: Why did you put a frog in your sister's bed?
Jimmy: I couldn't find a snake.

What's worse than finding a worm in your apple?
Finding half a worm.

"Waiter! There's a cockroach in my salad!"
"Please don't shout, sir. Or else the other customers will be asking for one, too!"

"Everything about life is funny."
—Monica Seles

Teacher: Oh dear! I've lost another pupil.
Principal: How did that happen?
Teacher: My glass eye flew out the window while I was driving.

Did you hear about the poor girl who swallowed the thermometer?
She's dying by degrees.

What's the difference between a saloon and an elephant's burp?
One is a bar room, and the other is a bar-OOOOM!

Do you remember when you lost your baby teeth?
Yeah, and was I surprised my dad could hit a baseball that hard!

"A train smashed into my bicycle, and I didn't even get hurt."
"Why not?"
"My brother Dave was riding it."

How do you keep a rooster from crowing on Sunday morning?
Make rooster stew Saturday night.

Why doesn't your sister like eating dill pickles?
She keeps getting her head stuck in the jar.

"That bully down the street just broke my finger!"
"Gosh, how did he do that?"
"He hit me in the nose."

Did you hear about the new principal who's been keeping the boys on their toes?
He raised all the urinals six inches.

How's Business?

Astronomer: It's looking up.

Submarine pilot: It has its ups and downs.

Oil rigger: Boring.

Tree doctor: Knot Two bad.

Carpenter: It's leveling off.

Surgeon: I always get a lot out of my patients.

Roofer: Customers are sliding off.

Boat racer: Sails are dropping.

Minister: Prophets are increasingly read.

Farmer: The field keeps growing.

Air traffic controller: Can't come, plane!

Model: The figures aren't all in yet.

Aerobics instructor: I'm reducing the bottom line.

How was King Henry VIII different from normal husbands?
He married his wives first, and axed them after.

There was a young monk of Siberia
Who of fasting grew wearia and wearia,
Till one day with a yell
He escaped from his cell
And devoured the Father Superia.

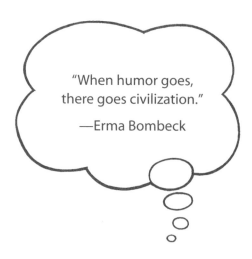

"When humor goes, there goes civilization."

—Erma Bombeck

Beekeeper: Business is humming.

Car mechanic: Planning to re-tire.

Pizza chef: Making dough hand over fist.

Miner: Roughly carving out a living.

Highway worker: A bit bumpy.

Ballet dancer: Keeps me on my toes.

Teacher: Sorry, but that's classified information!

JOKIN' AROUND

The Money Drop, or The Buck Doesn't Stop Here

Take out a crisp 1-dollar bill and hold it in your right hand. Let it hang down from your thumb and forefinger. Place the fingers and thumb of your left hand loosely around the bill without touching it. Let go of the bill with your right hand and catch it in your left hand. Don't grab it until the right hand has completely let go.

Show this little movement to your friends and bet them they can't catch the bill.

Again, hold the bill in your right hand. Let them (one at a time, of course) place their left hand loosely around the hanging bill. Tell them to catch the bill after you let go. Say, "If you can catch the falling bill, it's yours to keep."

They can't do it!

Why? In the time it takes your friends' eyeballs to register that the bill is falling, and for their brain to send out a second message to their hands telling them to grab, the bill has already dropped from their grasp. Gravity works too fast in this case, faster than human reflexes.

The reason you are able to catch the bill is because your brain knows when you are about to release the bill. Your friends, however, don't have that "insider" information.

Tips: The bill should be crisp. If it is not new, fold a crease in the bill lengthwise.

Instruct your friends not to grab the bill until they see you let go.

After practicing this trick, try it with a 10- or 20-dollar bill (if you dare!).

Having a Ball

What has 18 legs, spits, and catches flies?
A baseball team.

Why did the football coach rip apart the pay telephone?
He was trying to get his quarterback.

"The great comics and comedians have been the ones who dared to mix comedy with tragedy."

—Robin Tyler

(Who does Tyler think are great comics? Charlie Chaplin, Carol Burnett, Lily Tomlin, and Richard Pryor.)

Which football team travels with the most luggage?
The Packers.

What dessert should basketball players never eat?
Turnovers.

Which college team has the tallest players?
O-HIGH-O State.

Fullback: I'm sick, Coach. The doctor says I can't play football.
Coach: I don't need a doctor to tell me that!

Why is bowling cheaper than playing golf?
Because in bowling, no matter how badly you play, you can never lose the ball!

"What do you call your dad when he water skis in the winter?"
"A Popsicle."
"What does your mom call him?"
"Crazy!"

"Did you hear about the scuba diver who heard music underwater?"
"Was it a singing fish?"
"No, a coral group."

A college star fullback played with his team for 12 years!
He could run and tackle—he just couldn't pass.

What do you call a basketball player's pet chicken?
A personal fowl.

What do you get when a soccer player kicks a duck?
Someone who foots the bill.

Did you hear about the football coach who got his teeth knocked out?
He was showing a new player how to kick the ball. He held it on the ground and said, "Now when I nod my head, kick it!"

Golfer: Young man, why do you keep looking at your watch?
Caddie: This isn't a watch. It's a compass!

Did you hear about the billionaire who bought his kid 10 new golf clubs?
Each of them comes with a swimming pool and a private parking lot.

What is the quietest sport in the world?
Bowling. You can hear a pin drop.

What's the noisiest sport in the world?
Tennis. There's always a racket on the court.

Why is a baseball stadium such a cool place to be?
It's full of fans!

Did you hear about the quarterback who beat up his receiver every morning?
The quarterback gets up at six, and the receiver gets up at seven.

Golfer: Boy, the traps on this golf course are sure annoying.
Pro: I'll say, so would you please shut yours?

I heard there was a baseball team that won without ever putting a man on base.
Yeah, it was an all-girl team!

Angry Golfer: You must be the world's worst caddy!
Caddy: Oh no, that would be too much of a coincidence.

"There are two things the golf pro will not eat for breakfast."
"Really, what are they?"
"Lunch and dinner."

Why didn't the golfer wear his new shoes on the course today?
Because yesterday he got a hole in one.

Little Rosie was telling her friend about all the places her family had lived. "We must have lived in ten different towns since I was a baby." Her friend was impressed and asked, "Is your dad a minister or in the Army?" "Neither," said Rosie, "he's a football coach."

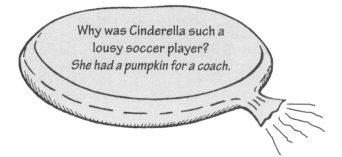

Why was Cinderella such a lousy soccer player? She had a pumpkin for a coach.

A fellow took his younger brother to the golf course with his pals. The younger boy thought he'd play his first game. He watched all the older boys tee off, and then stepped up to hit the ball.

"ONE!" he yelled, as he swung at the ball.

His brother rolled his eyes and said, "Why didn't you yell 'Fore' like the rest of us?"

The boy said, "You aim at whichever hole you want, I'm trying to hit the first one."

A mother brought her daughter to the golf course for the first time.

"What are those guys doing over there?" she asked her mother.

"They're checking out the sand traps."

"Cool, let's go see if they caught any."

Caddie: Here's a lost ball I found out on the course.
Boss: How do you know it was lost?
Caddie: Because they were still looking for it when I left.

Golfer: Any idea how I could cut about ten strokes off my game?
Caddie: Yeah, quit on the seventeenth hole.

"Everything is funny as long as it is happening to somebody else."

—Will Rogers

Video Quips (Punny Names)

Car Wars
directed by Otto Mobile

Cliff Hanger
directed by Ben Dover and Hugo First

I Was a Teenage Werewolf
directed by Anita Shave

Under the Bleachers
directed by Seymour Butts

Summer Vacation
directed by Sandy Beech

Explode!
directed by Adam Bomm

The Fortune Teller
directed by Horace Cope

Escape from New York
directed by Willy Makit

Escape from New York, Part Two
directed by Betty Will

Saved by the Bell
directed by Justin Tyme

JOKIN' AROUND

The Expanding Envelope

Tell your friends that you can walk through an envelope. That's right! *Through* an envelope. No one will believe you, but that's never stopped you before.

First, seal your envelope. Next, using scissors, carefully cut the envelope along the lines shown below. Cut into the body of the envelope and the sides … NOT the ends.

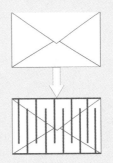

You will be able to carefully unfold your cut envelope into a much larger hoop. Step through the hoop. See, you've done it again!

Seeing Dead People
directed by Freyda Thudark

Who Wants To be a Zillionaire?
directed by Sherwood B. Nice.

The Pizza Guy
directed by Ann Chovey

Scary Movie
directed by Hans Archer Throte

Incredible Airplane Crashes!
directed by Isaac DeMye Stumick

Rock-and-Roll Prom
directed by Tristan Shout

The Last Video Game
directed by Joyce Tick

King of Comedy
directed by Shirley U. Jest

Lost Treasure
directed by Barry Deep

The Ghost Screams at Midnight
directed by Waylon Mone

Night of the Cat Burglar
directed by Jimmy DeLock

"The role of the comedian is to make the audience laugh, at a minimum of once every fifteen seconds."
—Lenny Bruce

Dinosaur Park
directed by Tara Dacktill

Revenge of the Mad Cow
directed by I. C. Hanz

Chickens Run
directed by Iona Farm

Return of the Zombies
directed by Doug Moregraves

All Those Dogs!
directed by Hunter and Juan del Mayshuns

Gags and Giggles

The dim-witted terrorist was sent out to blow up a car. He burned his lips on the exhaust pipe.

Two boys went to the movies. After the film had already started, they both got up and walked to the concession stand for some popcorn and soda pop. When they walked back into the darkened theater, one of the boys said to a man sitting on the aisle, "Excuse me, sir, but did we step on your toes on the way out?"

"You certainly did," said the man.

The boy turned to his friend and said, "Okay, this is our row."

There was the poor shoe salesman who had pulled out half of his stock, trying to find the perfect shoe for a young girl.

"Do you mind if I sit and rest a moment?" he asked her. "Your feet are killing me."

WORDS to KNOW

Gag: a laugh-provoking remark, trick, or prank

A snooty young woman was put off by a man begging for money.

"Are you satisfied walking the streets like this and asking for handouts?"

"No, ma'am," said the beggar. "I wish I could use a car."

Harry and his friends went deer hunting one fall. The first morning they all split up and disappeared into the woods. After lunch, Harry spotted one of his friends coming out of the woods.

"Where's the rest of the guys?" asked Harry, excitedly.

"They're at the cabin," said his friend.

"All of them?" asked Harry.

"Yeah, all of them."

"Are you sure?"

"Yes, Harry, I'm sure," said his friend. "Why do you keep asking?"

Harry had a big smile. "Boy, is that a relief. That means I shot a deer!"

Once the flood was over, Noah opened up the Ark and released all the animals back onto dry land. After the last animal had bounded off to freedom, Noah trudged wearily inside the ship to start the long chore of cleaning up. To his surprise, he noticed two snakes coiled up in a corner.

"Why are you two still here?" asked Noah.

One of the snakes answered, "Well, sir, you told us to go forth and multiply."

"Yes, indeed," said Noah.

"We can't multiply," said the snake. "We're adders."

A vampire took a vacation on a cruise ship. The headwaiter asked if he'd like to check out their menu.

"No thanks," said the vampire. "But do you have a passenger list?"

Gretchen: Why are you feeding your chickens boiled water?
Karl: I want them to lay boiled eggs.

Max: There's just one thing that would make you look even better than you do now.
Dot: What's that?
Max: Distance.

Did you hear about the knothead who fell down the elevator shaft?
When he gained consciousness he yelled, "I said UP!"

Rosie: Do you think my painting is any good?
Bill: In a way.
Rosie: What kind of way?
Bill: Away off.

A fellow walks into a hotel and asks for a room.

"We don't have any rooms," said the clerk. "We're full up."

"But I've been to every other hotel in this town," said the man. "They're all full. Are you sure you don't have any room somewhere?"

"I already told you," said the clerk. "No available room."

The man thought a moment then said, "If I were the president of the United States would you have a room for me?"

"Yes," said the clerk. "*If* you were the president."

"Well, give me *his* room, then," said the man, "Because he's not coming."

Did you hear about the rich kid whose father told him, "Son, I'm sorry, but tomorrow I need the limousine and chauffeur for work."

"But, Pop," said the kid, "how will I get to school?"

"Like every other normal kid in America," said the father. "You'll take a cab."

A prisoner on his way to the electric chair was asked if he had any last requests.

"I'd like some strawberries," says the prisoner.

"Strawberries?" says the guard. "They're not in season for six months yet."

The prisoner says, "Fine. I'll wait."

"We saw the Grand Canyon in ten days."
"That's a long vacation."
"Yeah, it took us five days to drive through and another five to refold the maps."

How did they measure hail before golf balls were invented?

"Are you sure you've ridden a horse before?"
"Oh yes."
"Then what kind of saddle would you like? With a horn or without?"
"I'll take the one without a horn. I doubt if I'll run into much traffic."

You heard what Noah told his son when they went fishing?
"Easy on the bait, son, we only have two worms."

A newspaper reporter was interviewing a gnarled, wrinkled, white-haired farmer as he sat quietly rocking on his front porch.

"Sir," said the reporter. "I'd like to know the secret of your long life."

"Well, son," replied the farmer. "I drink a gallon of whisky, smoke ten cigars, and stay out partying every night of the week."

"That's amazing," said the reporter. "And how old are you?"

"Twenty-six."

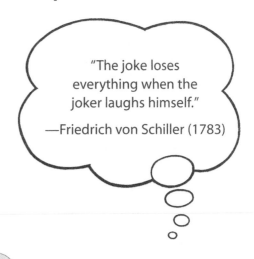

"The joke loses everything when the joker laughs himself."

—Friedrich von Schiller (1783)

JOKIN' AROUND

Bottom's Up

Bet your friends or family that you can drink from a soda pop can without opening it or tampering with it in any way. They'll think you're nuts! But you can prove them wrong.

Take a soda pop can and then turn it over. All aluminum pop cans have a slight indentation on the bottom. You can easily fill this indentation with water (or with pop from a different can). You'll be able to sip your drink from the can's bottom without opening it or tampering with it.

Tip: When making the bet, be sure to tell them that you will "drink *from* a can" and not "drink *out* of a can." The words are important. Say the wrong thing and your friends and family can trip you up, and you'll be forced to eat—or drink—your own words!

Mother: Honey, ask the butcher if he has calf's tongue.
Jimmy: Why ask? I'll just wait until he opens his mouth and look.

Mother (looking at the meat display): Jimmy, can you tell if the butcher has pickled pig's feet?
Jimmy: No, I can't. He's wearing shoes.

"Did you hear the news? They rescued a man from the swamp this morning whose foot was bitten off by an alligator!"
"Which one?"
"Who knows? All alligators look the same."

Have you heard about that new dog food?
It tastes like a mail carrier.

A rookie cop got bawled out by his sergeant after working his first stakeout.

"How could you let that crook escape?" yelled the sergeant. "I told you to keep an eye on all the exits."

"I did, Sarge. He must have gone out one of the entrances."

Did you hear about the weirdo who went to see a movie at the drive-in theater called *Closed for Repairs?*

The World's Seven Best Limericks

There was a young lady named Bright
Whose speed was much faster than light.
She went out one day
In a relative way
And came back on the previous night.

There was a young fellow of Crete
Who was so exceedingly neat,
When he got out of bed
He stood on his head
To make sure of not soiling his feet.

A flea and a fly in a flue
Were imprisoned so what could they do?
Said the fly, "Let us flee,"
Said the flea, "Let us fly,"
So they flew through a flaw in the flue.

There was a young lady of Niger
Who smiled as she rode on a tiger.
They returned from the ride
With the lady inside
And the smile on the face of the tiger.

A certain young man named Bill Beebee
Was in love with a lady named Phoebe
"But," he said, "we must see
What the clerical fee be
Before Phoebe be Phoebe Beebee."

There once was a maid from Japan
Whose limericks never would scan.
When they questioned her why,
She replied, "Because I
Like to squeeze as many syllables into the
concluding line of the limerick as I possibly can."

The bottle of perfume that Willie sent
Was highly displeasing to Millicent.
Her thanks were so cold
That they quarreled, I'm told,
'Bout that silly scent Willie sent Millicent.

FUN FACT

Briefly Funny

Limericks have been making people laugh for over a hundred years. But funny stuff can always be improved on. Comic poet Ogden Nash invented a streamlined, or mini version, of the Limerick called the **Limick**.

An outlaw from Spain
Fled to Paris by train
Where he jumped in the river—
They found him in-Seine.

A fellow from Hutton's,
The grandest of gluttons,
Makes room for dessert
By popping his buttons.

HA,HA,HA!

HA, HA, HA!

HA, HA, HA!

It's Rhyme Time

Add the missing letter in each of the following words to make a group of words that all rhyme. Now choose the three words that will correctly finish the limerick below. BE CAREFUL! Sometimes more than one letter can be used to make a word. If you can't find three words in your list that fit in the limerick, go back to the word list and try making other words.

B__Y   FR__
D__E   __YE
PI__   WH__
T__Y   __RY

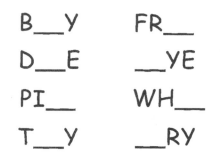

There was a young boy who asked,"_____
Can't I look in my ear with my_____?
If I put my mind to it,
I'm sure I could do it,
But I'll never know till I_____!"

Signs on the Dotty Line

Signs found hanging on the doors of . . .

An Astronaut: OUT TO LAUNCH
A fencing instructor: OUT TO LUNGE
A nuclear Scientist: GONE FISSION
A music Teacher: GONE CHOPIN, BE BACH SOON
A dance instructor: BACK IN A MINUET
A car mechanic: ON A BRAKE
A chiropractor: BE RIGHT, BACK!
A surgeon: JUST CUT OUT
A dog trainer: WILL RETURN IN FIVE MINUTES. SIT. STAY.
A nudist colony: WE'RE NEVER CLOTHED
A dentist: OPEN WIDE

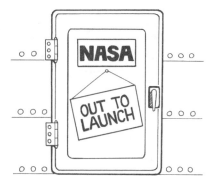

Bye Bye

Which sign did the eye doctor leave on her door when she went on vacation?

B	U	I	R
C R	B E	C U	U G
8 T V	G U D	L 8 R	R 8 2

Laughing Stock

"Does your family own a cat?"

"No, why?"

"I thought I heard it meowing last night."

"That's just our dog. He's been listening to foreign language tapes."

Jenny: Doctor, I have a problem. I love Bermuda shorts.

Doctor: Lots of people love Bermuda shorts.

Jenny: With mustard and relish?

"I got a role in the new *Tarzan* movie. Boy, you should have seen all the crazy animals we had to work with."

"Were you the star?"

"No, but when the lion got loose and chased the cast, I was the leading man!"

"The best humor is the most obvious. When the audience has to stop and think too hard about a punchline, the punch is lost."

—Thom Melcher

Harold and Stanley were brothers. Harold went on a business trip and asked Stanley to look after his pet kitten. The first night of his trip, Harold phoned his brother and asked how little Buttons was doing.

"Buttons is dead," said Stanley, flatly.

Harold was appalled. "Stanley! That's no way to tell me bad news."

"How should I have told you?" asked Stanley.

"Break it to me gently," said Harold. "Little by little. You could have said that Buttons was up on the roof. Then say you had to call the fire department. Then say the ladder wasn't long enough. Then tell me that Buttons tried to jump. And then you could have said he was in the hospital. And that he was growing weaker and weaker. That he stopped eating. Then, eventually, you could have told me that poor Buttons died."

"Sorry," said Stanley. "I'll know better next time."

"All right," said Harold. "By the way, how's Mom?"

"Well, she's up on the roof."

A miser won the lottery with a ticket he bought—$1,000,000! But he still seemed depressed. "What's wrong?" asked his neighbor. The miser sighed and said, "When I think of the dollar I *wasted* buying this other lottery ticket."

Joey: Yuck! This is the worst tasting apple pie I ever had!

Waiter: What does it taste like?

Joey: Glue!

Waiter: Then that's the pumpkin pie. The apple pie tastes like mud.

Mother: Billy, what is all that grass doing sticking out of your pockets?

Billy: The worms in there have to eat something, don't they?

Troop Leader: Do you know how to make a fire with just two sticks?

Cub Scout: Yes, sir. As long as one of the sticks is a match.

My poor sister had an awful time of it. First she got arthritis and rheumatism. And after that she got appendicitis, tonsillitis, and then pneumonia. They even had to give her hypodermics. Whew! I didn't think she'd ever make it through that spelling contest!

Five-year-old Kevin came running down the stairs, wailing and weeping. "What ever is the matter?" asked his mother. "I was upstairs with Daddy," said Kevin. "He was putting up pictures. And he hit his thumb with the hammer." The mother grinned. "That's all right, honey. Your daddy is a grown-up man. He doesn't let something like that worry him. And you shouldn't either. You should have just laughed." Then Kevin sobbed, "I did!"

My doctor believes in shock therapy. That's why he sends me his bill!

"Excuse me, could you tell me the fastest way to get to the hospital?"

"Stand in traffic."

"I was thinking of attending the time-management workshop."

"When does it start?'

"Oh, fivish, sixish."

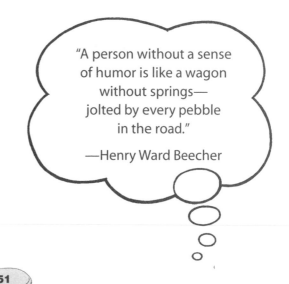

"A person without a sense of humor is like a wagon without springs— jolted by every pebble in the road."

—Henry Ward Beecher

A man walked into an antique store. It was filled with beautiful furniture, fine old paintings, and housewares of silver and crystal. Nothing caught his eye. As he turned to leave, however, he noticed the owner's cat licking milk out of a delicate china saucer. The man knew at a glance that the saucer was priceless, and he figured the stupid owner didn't realize what a treasure was sitting just beneath his nose.

The man casually struck up a conversation with the owner.

"Nice cat you got there."

"Thanks," said the owner. "He's a good cat, but I never seem to have enough time for him."

"Hmmm, would you be interested in selling him?" asked the man.

"Sure, if you're serious," said the owner. "You can have him for five bucks."

"Deal."

The man paid his five dollars, then picked up the cat and headed toward the door. "Oh, by the way," said the man, turning around. "You probably wouldn't mind if I just took that old milk saucer would you? The cat seems to like it."

"Are you kidding?" grinned the man. "That saucer has helped me sell seventy cats in the last month!"

"I'm on that new Japanese diet."
"How does that work?"
"You're only allowed to use one chopstick."

A doctor walks into a hospital room and stands next to the bed of his patient.

"Mister Cooper, I have some good news and some bad news."

"What is it, Doc?"

"The bad news is that we have to amputate both your feet."

"That's horrible! What's the good news?"

"The patient in the next bed wants to buy your shoes."

Picto-Laugh #3

A pictograph is a very simple drawing of something funny. Can you guess what this little picto-laugh is showing? HINT: Think about Mexican hats and exercise!

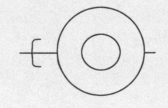

First Scientist: I discovered the perfect cure for dandruff.
Second Scientist: What is it?
First Scientist: Baldness.

Years ago, a huge ship was passing through a thick fog. Suddenly, up ahead, it saw a bright and unexpected light. The ship signaled: "Veer off!"

The reply: "You veer off!"

The captain of the ship became furious. He told his signal man, "Tell that idiot to veer off! Doesn't he realize this battleship is heading his way?"

The signal man obeyed the command and then waited for a reply.

"Well, what did he say?" asked the angry captain.

The signal man answered, "Well, sir, he says, 'Don't you realize this lighthouse is heading *your* way?'"

Harold got a summer job painting yellow stripes down the middle of the highway. The first day he did an excellent job and painted a strip a mile long. But the second day he painted only half a mile. And the third day Harold painted even less.

Finally, his angry boss told him, "Harold, you're slacking off! Each day you paint less and less."

Harold replied, "I know. But each day it gets longer and longer to walk back to that bucket!"

Love To Laugh

A good joke can make you laugh out loud or quietly to yourself. See if you can fill in five different kinds of laughs. We left a couple of L-A-U-G-H-S to help you.

Hint: a little girl's laugh

Hint: a big, belly laugh

Hint: Sounds like the name of a candy bar!

Hint: a quiet, private laugh

Hint: A witch's laugh

"I don't have a penny to my name."
"Are you gonna get a job?"
"No, I'm gonna change my name."

Did you hear about the elephant hunter who hurt his back?
He was carrying decoys.

A miser walks into a dentist's office and asks the dentist how much he charges for pulling a tooth.

"Thirty bucks," said the dentist.

"Here's five," said the miser. "Just loosen it a little."

A young girl entered the courthouse and registered for a name change.

"What's your name now?" asked the clerk.

"Betty Stinks," said the girl.

The clerk laughed for almost a full minute. "I can understand why you'd want to change it," the clerk finally said. "What are you changing it to?"

"Elizabeth Stinks."

First Fisher: Is this a good lake for fish?
Second Fisher: It must be. I can't get any of them to come out.

Two cars, driving from opposite directions, met in the middle of a narrow bridge that was wide enough to let only one car pass at a time.

The first motorist rolled down his window, stuck his head out, and yelled, "I never back up for jerks!"

The second driver put his car in reverse and yelled, "That's all right. I always do!"

Picto-Laugh #4

A pictograph is a very simple drawing of something funny. Can you guess what this little picto-laugh is showing? HINT: Think about Mexican hats and breakfast!

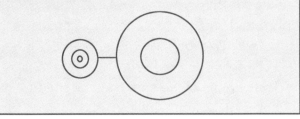

"I want to see Dr. Braun."

"He's not here at the moment. But I'm sure Dr. Wilson could help you."

"I don't want Dr. Wilson. I want Dr. Braun."

"Then you'll just have to wait."

"Fine. How long?"

"Two weeks. Dr. Braun just left on his vacation."

A mother raced into a doctor's office, pulling her son along behind her. "Tell me, Doctor," she said, "can a ten-year-old boy take out a person's appendix?"

"Don't be ridiculous," said the doctor. "Of course not."

"See, Jimmy? You heard the doctor. Now go put that right back!"

Jimmy: This is the slowest train I've ever been on! Conductor, can't you run any faster?
Conductor: Sure I can. But I have to stay on the train.

Larry: Why don't we fall off the earth and go shooting through space?

Perry: The law of gravity.

Larry: Then what did we do before that law was passed?

A young girl walked into a clothing store with her mother. "I'd like to try on that dress in the window," she said.

"Well, young lady," said the clerk, "we'd prefer that you use one of our dressing rooms."

Jimmy: How's your new job on the construction site?

Derek: Awful! After one week, I'm through with it!

Jimmy: What for?

Derek: Lots of reasons. The constant complaining, the laziness, the sloppiness, the bad language. They just wouldn't put up with it anymore!

It's Joke Time!

Draw a line from each riddle to the clock that shows the correct answer.
HINT: It helps to read the time on each clock aloud.

What time is it when five tigers are chasing you?

What time is it when you have a toothache?

What time is it when baseball teams have a tie score?

What time is the same backward or forward?

Pundemonium

I heard on the news that a nuclear scientist accidentally ate some uranium, and now he has atomic ache!

"How's your sister coming along with her new jigsaw puzzle?"
"She can't figure it out. I'm afraid she's going to pieces."

Did you hear they fired the cross-eyed school teacher?
He couldn't control his pupils.

Did you hear about the lobster that bought a new car?
It was a crustacean wagon.

"Does your brother have a job?"
"He works at the hospital as a night orderly."
"Oh, a pan-handler, huh?"

Pun: the humorous use of a word in such a way as to suggest two or more of its meanings or the meaning of another word with a similar sound

Doctor: Have your eyes ever been checked?
Kyle: No, they've always been blue.

What did one Moroccan boy say to the other?
"I can't remember your name, but your fez is familiar."

A misshapen ogre made his living by ringing the bells at a famous cathedral in France. One day the ogre lost his footing on the roof of the cathedral and plummeted 200 feet to his death in the courtyard below. Two priests rushed to the ogre's side. The first priest asked, "Is that the Hunchback of Notre Dame?" The second priest replied, "No, but he's a dead ringer."

Tyler: My dad is so strong, he can hold up several cars at once using one hand.

Brian: What does he do?

Tyler: He's a policeman.

Brian: Big deal! My dad is a lot stronger. He can hold up an entire bank by just handing a little note to the teller.

What's the best way to avoid falling hair?
Jump out of the way!

Dottie was having trouble learning her directions, especially the difference between north and south. So her mother tried a little quiz. "Dottie, if you were standing with your back to the east, and your face to the west, what would be on your right hand?"

Dottie said, "Four fingers and a thumb."

Teacher: My goodness, Amy! You've been burping all morning.

Amy: It must have been those belchin' waffles I ate for breakfast.

Matty: We learned today that people who live north of the Arctic Circle eat whale meat and blubber.

Mary: I'd blubber too if that's all I had to eat.

Mom: Amy, what are you doing home from school so early?

Amy: The teacher asked me how far I could count, so I counted all the way home.

"My aunt always nagged my uncle to buy her a Jaguar."
"Did he ever get one?"
"Yeah, then it ate her up!"

Circus Clown: How do you like your new job?

Trapeze Artist: I'm finally getting the hang of things.

How do you measure a dog's temperature?
By pedigrees.

Some know-it-all once said that the *pun* was the lowest form of humor. Then a modern comic added, "unless you happen to make it yourself!"

I feel sorry for the two lighthouse keepers.
Their marriage is on the rocks.

Young earthworm: This dirt tastes terrible.
Mother earthworm: I don't understand. It was
fresh ground this morning.

You heard about the glass blower who
inhaled?
He got a pane in his stomach.

What did the Cub Scout say when he fixed the
horn on his bike?
Beep repaired!

Why does your dog go round and round
before he lies down?
He's a self-winding watchdog.

A music store was robbed last night. The
burglar broke in, stole a drum, and beat it!

Why is that woolly sheep scratching itself?
Because it has fleece.

"Comedy is the new
rock-and-roll."

—Janet Street-Porter

Teacher: Alex, why are you brushing your teeth
during class?
Alex: I want to be ready for the oral exam.

Did you hear about the two silkworms who had
a race?
They ended in a tie.

That movie was terrible. I've seen a better film
on dirty teeth.

Why did the bank robber flee to the nudist
colony?
That's where he had his hide out.

What do you see when the smog clears in
southern California?
U.C.L.A.

What part of a car is responsible for causing
the most accidents?
The nut located behind the wheel.

Clueless Kids

They think that . . .

An octopus is a cat with eight paws.

A polygon is a parrot who flew from its cage.

An amoeba is a small prison, because it only has one cell.

Peanut butter is a baby billy goat.

Shell-shock is when you accidentally drop an egg.

"Doctor, can you help me? I keep thinking I'm a packet of biscuits."
"Biscuits? Oh, you mean those little square packets you crumble up for your soup?"
"Yes, exactly."
"Then you must be crackers!"

"You look awful, Stanley. Flu?"
"Yeah, and crashed!"

I read that Tibet is the noisiest place on earth.
Everywhere you look it's Yak, Yak, Yak!

Did you hear about the Siamese twins who went to Prague for major surgery?
They came out as separate Czechs.

"This report card should be underwater!"
"Because it's so wet?"
"No, because it's below "C" level!"

What happened to the origami store that used to be on the corner?
It folded.

An inexperienced hunter was deep in the woods and kept following a set of tracks—until the train ran him over!

Picto-Laugh #5

A pictograph is a very simple drawing of something funny. Can you guess what this little picto-laugh is showing? HINT: Think about the color pink!

Fill Me In

Color in all the shapes with exactly three sides to find the answer to this riddle: Why did Silly Billy throw a stick of butter out the window?

Why did Silly Billy throw a stick of butter out of the window?

Karl: Darn, I left my watch back up on that hill.
Ben: Should we go up and get it?
Karl: Nah, it'll run down by itself.

Gretchen: Every morning my dog and I go for a tramp in the woods.
Heather: Sounds delightful.
Gretchen: Yes, but the tramp is getting real tired of it.

At a fancy hotel, a man walks in and asks the desk clerk, "Do you take children?"

"No sir," replied the clerk. "Only checks and American Express."

The farmer came in from the barn and said to his wife:

"I shot the cow."

"Was he a mad cow?"

"Let's just say he wasn't too happy about it."

A once-famous rock star told her friend, "The last time I made an appearance at that nightclub, I drew a line five blocks long."

Her friend asked, "Did they make you erase it?"

"I think I have a good head on my shoulders."
"You sure have a point there."

Why do you keep a sun lamp in your lunchbox? *It's a light lunch.*

Funny Business

Did you realize that if 3M and Goodyear ever merged they could call themselves MMMGood?

And if Polygram Records, Warner Brothers, and Nabisco Crackers ever joined forces, they would be called Poly-Warner-Cracker.

A Pun-oply for Pun Lovers

Here's an alphabetical list of old or obsolete words that all mean "pun." Some of these words are over 500 years old!

bull
carrawitchet
clinch
crotchet
figary
flim
jerk
liripoop
pundigrion
quarterquibble
quillet
quirk
sham
whim

If you always have a pun up your sleeve that you can't wait to try out on your friends, you are said to be "liripoopionated."

And if you pun way too much, your friends can accuse you of "quibble-ism."

Nuts from the Family Tree

Mother: What's the best way to discipline
children?
Father: Start at the bottom.

Ashley: Everyone says I got my good looks
from my father.
Jason: Oh, is he a plastic surgeon?

"My older brother thinks he's a chicken."
"You should take him to a doctor."
"Why? We need the eggs."

"We got a dog
for my little brother."
"I wish my Dad would let me
make a trade like that."

Mother: Darling, will you still love me when my
hair is gray?
Father: Why not? I loved you through those five
other colors.

At the airport, Mother turned to Father and
said, "I sure wish we had brought the
television with us."
   "Why is that?" asked Father.
   "Because I left the plane tickets on it."

Karl and Ben went out hunting. They were just
bedding down in their tents one night when a
huge snarling bear lumbered into their
campsite. Karl quickly knelt down and started
lacing up his sneakers.
   "What good will that do?" shouted Ben.
"You can't outrun a bear."
   Karl replied, "I only have to outrun *you!*"

A very proud grandmother was walking
through the park, pushing her two
grandchildren in a stroller. A
young woman walked by
and said, "My, what
fine looking little
boys. They must be
your grandsons." "Yes
they are," said the
grandmother. "How old
are they?" asked the
younger woman. "The
lawyer is three and the
doctor is two."

Jason: What's it like having a twin sister?
Megan: It's just like being an only child. Except twice.

"Mom, guess what? I won the election for class president!"
"Honestly?"
"Did you have to bring that up?"

"Humor has to come in under cover of darkness, in disguise, and surprise people."

—Garrison Keillor

"Dad, where is yesterday's newspaper?"
"Your mother wrapped the garbage in it and threw it away."
"Darn, I wanted to see it."
"There wasn't much to see. Just some old egg cartons and dogfood cans and apple cores and . . ."

"My dad used to write for TV. He wrote *The Jeffersons, The Hughleys,* and *The PJ's.*"
"Did they ever write back?"

"I can always tell when my big brother is lying."
"How's that?"
"He moves his lips."

"What are you having for dinner tonight?"
"Reruns."
"Reruns?"
"Yeah, leftover TV dinners."

"My brother made a right turn from the left lane and crashed into another car. The other driver jumped out and yelled at my brother. Why didn't you signal? he asked."
"What did your brother say?"
"He said, 'Why should I signal? I always turn here.'"

My Dad is a real pessimist. He just opened up a new Chinese restaurant and he only sells *misfortune* cookies.

"Doctor, my sister thinks she's an elevator. Can you help her?"
"Have her come up to my office."
"I would, but she doesn't stop at your floor."

"George Washington's parents were really thoughtful."
"What makes you say that?"
"They made sure their kid was born on a holiday."

Troy: Mom! Megan said I was dumb.
Mother: Megan, apologize to your brother!
Megan: Okay. I'm sorry you're dumb.

"My sister loves to eat."
"What's her favorite food?"
"Seconds."

Troy: Your piano playing stinks!
Megan: Well, for your information, that piece I was playing is very difficult.
Troy: Too bad it's not impossible.

"My brother is connected with the police."
"How's he connected?"
"With handcuffs."

Alex: My dad lost his wallet with over three hundred bucks in it.
Troy: Wow!
Alex: And he's offering a reward of twenty dollars to whoever finds it.
Troy: I'll give you thirty.

Three comedians were asked which is funnier: a witty line or someone slipping on a banana peel. Fran Lebowitz and Ellen DeGeneres both said that falling down is funnier. Lily Tomlin said it "depends on who's doing the slipping."

Amy: Dad, the landlord is here for the rent.
Father: Tell him I'm not home.
Amy: I can't lie like that!
Father: All right, I'll tell him myself.

Alex: Mom, I think it's time I got an allowance.
Mother: How about I give you double what I give your little brother, Matt?
Alex: But Matt gets zero allowance.
Mother: Okay, so I'll give you triple.

A young boy was telling his teacher all about the new addition to his family. "And every night," complained the boy, "little Kevin wakes everyone up with his crying."
   "Well, he's just a wee little thing," said the teacher.
   "No," said the boy. "He's a wee-wee thing. That's why he's crying."

Mother: Why did you kick your little brother in the stomach?
Jimmy: He turned around.

Teacher: How do you make antifreeze?
Rosie: Steal her blanket.

The real-estate agent told the family, "I'll be honest with you. This house has its good points as well as its bad points."

"What are the bad points?" asked the father.

"Just north of here is a toxic waste dump. And just south is a huge hog farm."

"What are the good points?" asked the mother.

"You can always tell which way the wind is blowing."

In the middle of a sweltering summer afternoon, the Thomas family was entertaining out-of-town guests. When supper was ready, the father asked the youngest son to say the blessing.

The boy whispered to his father, "But what do I say?"

The father replied, "Just say what you've heard me say before."

So the boy bowed his head and said in a loud voice, "Oh Lord, why in heaven's name did I ever invite these people on a hot day like today?"

Jimmy: My sister thinks I'm too nosy.
Troy: Did she tell you that?
Jimmy: No, that's what I read in her diary.

"What are you drawing, honey?"
"A picture of God."
"But no one knows what God looks like."
"They will when I'm finished with this."

"My brother has laryngitis, so he's talking with his hands."
"Is that why he's snapping his fingers?"
"Yeah, he has the hiccups."

Danny: Guess what, Dad? Mom backed the car out of the garage and ran right over my new bike.
Father: That'll teach you to leave it parked out on the front lawn.

"Young man, there were two cookies in the jar last night, and this morning there is only one. How do you explain that?"
"It was so dark, I guessed I missed it."

My mom gets carsickness every month—when she looks at the payment.

Mother: Rosie! Why did you fall in the mud puddle with your new dress on?
Rosie: There wasn't time to take it off.

Father: I think our son must get his brains from me.
Mother: Probably, because I still have all mine.

Matt: Dad! The dog just ate the pie Mom finished baking.
Father: That's all right, son, don't worry. We'll get you a new dog.

Did you hear about the nervous father who is pacing up and down in the hospital lobby, waiting to hear about the birth of his first child? Finally, after several hours, the nurse arrives. The father runs up to her and asks, "Nurse, tell me, is it a boy?" The nurse says calmly, "Well, the middle one is."

Mother: Boys, stop fighting! Who started this anyway?
Nick: Matt started it when he hit me back.

Aunt Missy: Do you know what an opera is, Rosie?
Rosie: Yeah, it's where someone gets stabbed and instead of bleeding they sing.

A grandmother took her little five-year-old grandson with her shopping. At one point in the store the little boy said loudly, "I have to go pee-pee." The grandmother shook her head and said, "No, dear. When you need to use the bathroom you say that you have *to whisper.* All right?"

That night the five-year-old woke up at midnight and toddled into his parents' bedroom. "Daddy," he said, tugging on his father's arm, "I have to whisper! I have to whisper!"

The father sleepily turned over on his side and said, "All right, son. Go ahead and whisper right in my ear."

Picto-Laugh #6

A pictograph is a very simple drawing of something funny. Can you guess what this little picto-laugh is showing? HINT: Think about a game of hide-n-seek!

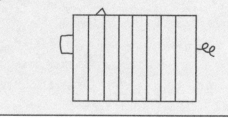

"My sister ran the hundred-yard dash in five seconds."

"That's impossible! The world record isn't even eight seconds."

"She knows a short cut."

"Do you have to make so much noise when you eat?"

"Our teacher told us to start the day with a sound breakfast."

Ben: Why are you jumping up and down?

Karl: I just took some medicine, and the bottle said to shake well.

"You sure take your car in for lots of repairs."

"I know, my dad is always braking it."

Mother: Why are you standing in front of the mirror with your eyes shut?

Melody: I want to see what I look like asleep.

Rhyming Riddles

Draw a line to match each riddle to the proper picture.

It keeps you nice and very neat—has lots of teeth, but cannot eat.

It runs all night, and runs all day, but never, ever runs away.

Sits on the table by your plate and cup—if it falls down, it might stick up.

Sometimes curly, sometimes flat—it's over the head and under a hat.

• •

"My dad only eats at the finest restaurants."

"How do you know that?"

"You should see our silverware."

Father: Go right up to your room and straighten it.

Jimmy: Is it crooked?

JOKIN' AROUND

The Woman on the Bus

A woman was riding the bus downtown with her new baby.

A rude passenger sitting across the aisle took one look at the woman and her baby and said, "That's the ugliest baby I ever saw in my life. Looks just like a monkey." The woman was so upset that she quickly got off the bus at the very next stop. She walked over to a park bench, sat down, and started crying.

A young man walking by noticed the poor woman. "What's wrong?" he asked her. But the woman was too upset to tell him. It was a hot day out, so the man walked over to a convenience store and a few minutes later returned to the park bench.

The young man handed the woman a can of soda pop. "It's so hot out, I thought you might like this," he said. The woman gratefully accepted his offer. "Thank you very much," she said. Then the man reached into his pocket. "Here, take this," he said. "I bought a banana for your monkey, too."

"Why aren't you sharing your scooter with your little brother?"

"I am, Mom, half and half. I use it on the way down the hill, and he has it on the way up the hill."

Heather: I just finished giving my kitten a bath.
Tracy: Does she mind it?
Heather: No, she likes it. But afterwards it always takes me a while to get rid of the fur on my tongue.

Mother:
What a dirty face! Your Aunt Missy won't kiss you like that.
Alex: That's what I figured.

Mother: What's your little brother yelling about?
Sandy: I don't know. I let him lick the beater after I made peanut butter fudge. Maybe I should have turned it off first.

A young boy, taking a vacation cruise with his parents, turned green with seasickness.

"Are you sure you don't want dinner, honey?" asked his mother.

The boy shook his head and replied, "Just throw it overboard, Mom, and save me the trip to the railing."

You Know You're a Loser When . . .

✔ Your ship comes in and you're at the train station.

✔ Your talking mynah bird says, "Who asked you?"

✔ Your twin forgets your birthday.

✔ Your parents attend PTA meetings under an assumed name.

✔ Your answering machine hangs up on you.

Spoonerisms

The Reverend William Archibald Spooner (1844–1930) of Oxford University in England was famous for getting his tongue tied. Instead of saying "Our Lord is a loving shepherd," Spooner called him a "shoving leopard." Instead of sitting on a "stone bench," he'd relax on a "bone stench." Spoonerism is now the name we give a gag or phrase where the first letters of a word are exchanged for another. Below are some of the Reverend's sillier blunders.

• He whispered to a young man in an overcrowded church: "Excuse me, sir, but you're occupewing my pie. May I sew you to another sheet?"

• He told a tardy student: "You have hissed all my mystery lectures!"

• To a group of farmers, he started a speech by saying: "I have never before spoken to so many tons of soil."

• After performing a wedding ceremony, he then instructed the nervous groom: "It is kisstomary to cuss the bride."

WORDS to KNOW

Spoonerism: a phrase where the first letters of a word are exchanged for another

Here's a few more tongue stumblers:

"I need to buy a new can of oderarm deunderant."

"This fog is as thick as sea poop."

"Drinking lots of coffee always weeps me a cake."

"In New York Harbor, my uncle supervises all the bug totes."

"While I run into the shandy cop, would you keep your buy on my icicle?"

What's The Difference?

These riddles ask you to tell the difference between two things. The answer is always a pair of words. When you read the words one way, they describe the first thing in the riddle. When you switch the pair of words around, they describe the second thing! See if you can choose the correct pairs of words that will complete each riddle. Write your answers in the spaces provided. The first one has been half done for you!

1. What's the difference between a rain gutter and a clumsy baseball player?

   (One catches drops, and the other _____.)

2. What's the difference between a fake dollar bill and a crazy rabbit?

   (One is _____, and the other is a_____.)

3. What's the difference between a jail warden and a jeweler?

   (One _____, and the other _____.)

4. What's the difference between a sneaky student and a mouse?

   (One is a_____, and the other is a _____.)

5. What's the difference between a bowl of moldy lettuce and a depressing song?

   (One is a_____, and the other is a _____.)

6. What's the difference between a healthy rabbit and a bad joke?

   (One is a_____, and the other is only a _____.)

PAIRS TO CHOOSE FROM:

sells watches

cheesy eater

drops catches

bad salad

fit bunny

mad bunny

watches cells

sad ballad

bad money

easy cheater

bit funny

A Spoonerful of Tea (a True Story)

The Reverend Spooner met a stranger while strolling through the university grounds one evening.

Spooner: Come to my place for tea tomorrow, young man. We're having a welcome party for the new math professor.

Stranger: But I am the new math professor.

Spooner: That's all right. Come anyway.

Spooner's Bug

Q: What spoonerism has become a common word that refers to something we see during the summer months?

A: Butterfly. The insect was once known as a *flutter-by*, named for its fluttery, delicate movement.

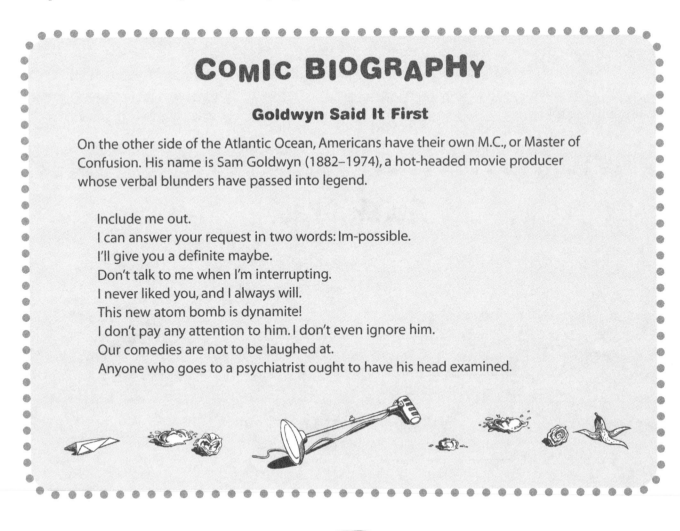

COMIC BIOGRAPHY

Goldwyn Said It First

On the other side of the Atlantic Ocean, Americans have their own M.C., or Master of Confusion. His name is Sam Goldwyn (1882–1974), a hot-headed movie producer whose verbal blunders have passed into legend.

Include me out.
I can answer your request in two words: Im-possible.
I'll give you a definite maybe.
Don't talk to me when I'm interrupting.
I never liked you, and I always will.
This new atom bomb is dynamite!
I don't pay any attention to him. I don't even ignore him.
Our comedies are not to be laughed at.
Anyone who goes to a psychiatrist ought to have his head examined.

Nun of That

A new nun joined a special order where all the sisters had to take a vow of silence. Only two words were allowed each sister per year. After the first year, the Mother Superior asked the newest nun how things were going.

"Bad food," said the nun.

The next year the Mother Superior asked the nun the same question.

"Hard beds," said the nun.

At the end of the third year, the nun walked up to the Mother Superior and said, "I quit!"

"Well I'm not surprised," said the Mother Superior. "Ever since you got here you've done nothing but complain."

"That is the best—to laugh with someone because you think the same things are funny."

—Gloria Vanderbilt

Nun: Remember, young lady, we are in this world to help others.
Melody: Okay, but what are the others here for?

Quick Draw

These funny drawings show the names of three common things. Can you guess what each is?

Way-Out Out West (Cowboy Jokes)

A cowboy was riding his horse one day when he accidentally got thrown off. The quick-thinking horse pulled the cowboy to a shady oasis, propped him up against a tree, and then galloped off for help. He soon returned with some folks from a neighboring town, including a doctor. The doctor and the others brought the cowboy into town and nursed him back to full health.

A week later, when the cowboy was telling his buddies at the saloon this story, one of them said, "That's the gol-dang smartest horse I ever heard tell of."

"Aw, he ain't that smart," said the cowboy. "The doctor he brung with him was a vet."

A cowboy bought a beautiful new horse. The salesman told him that the horse's former owner had been a famous preacher.

"This horse is very religious," said the salesman. "And he only responds to special commands. For instance, instead of saying Giddy-up, you say Praise the Lord. And instead of telling him to Whoa! you say Hallelujah. Got that?"

"Praise the Lord and Hallelujah," nodded the cowboy.

Weeks later, the cowboy was riding through unfamiliar territory. Gorges and cliffs fell hundreds of feet on either side of the trail. The cowboy wanted to stop and take a rest, but he confused the two words the salesman had taught him.

"Praise the Lord," the cowboy said, but the horse kept on galloping faster and faster. The cowboy saw that the trail up ahead ended in a dangerous cliff. He tugged and pulled at the reins even harder and yelled, "Praise the Lord! Praise the Lord!" but the horse continued to race toward the cliff.

All at once, the cowboy remembered the right word.

"Hallelujah!" he cried.

The horse immediately stopped, mere inches from the crumbling edge of the cliff.

The cowboy breathed a sigh of relief and pulled off his hat, wiping the dust from his eyes.

"Praise the Lord," he said.

JOKIN' AROUND

Turtle Soup

Three little turtles, who lived in the same house together, were having Sunday dinner. They each sipped their own bowl of soup.

"This soup would sure taste better with some bread," said the first turtle.

"We're all out of bread," said the second turtle.

"Well, I'm not going to the store," said the third, and littlest, turtle. "If I go, you two will eat my soup."

The other two turtles promised him they would never touch his soup. "Go to the store and hurry back," said the first turtle. So the littlest turtle reluctantly walked out the door.

Minutes stretched into hours. Hours stretched into days. A week later, the turtles were still waiting for their friend to return from the store with the bread.

The first turtle said, "I don't think he's ever coming back. We might as well go ahead and have his soup."

Just then, the littlest turtle poked his head back inside the door. "See?" he said. "I knew if I left you guys would eat my dinner!"

Money Is only Paper

Tallulah Bankhead (1903–1968) was a flamboyant actress known for her generosity as well as for saying whatever popped into her head. Once when Tallulah was using a lady's bathroom, sitting in a stall, she realized there was no toilet paper.

She called over to the next stall, "Have you any toilet paper, darling?"

"No, I'm afraid not."

"Hmm, any tissue paper?"

"Sorry, no."

Tallulah paused and then asked calmly, "Have you two fives for a ten?"

A Nutty Crime

A judge had three young boys come before his bench.

The first boy said, "All I did, Your Honor, was break a window, wreck someone's bike, and throw peanuts in the lake."

The second boy said, "Me too, Your Honor. I only broke a small window, wrecked a friend's bike, and threw peanuts in the lake."

The third boy said, "All I did was break a window and wreck a bike."

The judge turned to the third boy and said, "Didn't you throw peanuts in the lake?"

The boy said, "I'm Peanuts."

More Nuts

A man walks into a fancy bar and orders a glass of wine. It's early evening and the bar has only a few customers.

The man hears a voice next to him say, "Nice tie." The man looks around, but there is no one sitting nearby. He figures he must be hearing things.

He takes a sip of wine and hears, "I like that suit you're wearing." Again, the man swivels around on his chair but sees no one.

Another sip of wine and the man hears, "That blue shirt really brings out your eyes."

"Okay!" says the man. "That does it! What's going on, and who keeps talking to me?"

The bartender, unfazed, looks over at the man and says, "It's just the peanuts, mister. They're complimentary."

Pretty Funny

Have you ever noticed how few handsome men or beautiful women are comedians? There are a few exceptions: Cary Grant, Carole Lombard, Tom Selleck, Cybill Shepherd, Julia-Louis Dreyfus. Woody Allen, the director of *Sleeper*, *Bullets Over Broadway*, *Bananas*, and *Annie Hall*, has his own theory. "Funny and pretty are opposites," he says. But the standup comic Mort Sahl has a different idea. He enjoyed telling jokes, he says, because to him "people always look better when they laugh."

Bruce Vilanch, the incredibly busy Hollywood writer, widely known for his stint as the big, blond funnyman on *Hollywood Squares*, shares this advice about writing comedy: "Rewriting is really what good writing is all about!" Asked if there is any subject he would not write a joke about, Vilanch replies: "My rule of thumb is, did anybody die? It's difficult to do a joke in which death is involved ... it's just cruel."

Classic One-Liners

A one-liner is a joke that is told in one line or sentence. Or else several phrases are strung together and spoken without a break. For example: My room is so small . . .

I closed the door and the doorknob was in bed with me.

the mice are hunchbacked.

when I turn around, I'm next door.

I put the key in the keyhole and broke the window.

I have to go outside to change my mind.

when I stand up I'm on the second floor.

the ceiling gets dusted whenever I comb my hair.

One-liner: a joke that is told in one line or sentence

More One-Liners

A mummy is an Egyptian who's pressed for time.

I saw a sign on the back of a truck: "Careful Passing. I Like to Chew Tobacco."

I'm a terrible cook. All the gingerbread boys I make are nearsighted so I've started using contact raisins.

What do you get if you cross a hill with an electric stove?
A mountain range.

My mom went to the beauty salon and got a mud pack—for three days she looked great—then the mud fell off.

The standup comic Henny Youngman is called the King of the One-Liners. Rodney Dangerfield and Steven Wright are also terrific one-line jokesters. Here's one of Wright's loopy one-liners: "I live on a one-way, dead-end street. I don't know how I got there."

Medical Marvels

Pump Up the Laughter

Did you know that by simply telling a joke you are exercising 72 different muscles in your neck, throat, mouth, and tongue? Laughing uses over 100 muscles. No wonder some people say they "laughed 'til they hurt." They just had a workout without even realizing it!

A Joke a Day Keeps the Doctor Away

Dr. Lee Berk of the Loma Linda School of Public Health in California discovered that laughing increases the body's antibodies and T cells, which help fight off infection and alien bacteria.

Dr. William Fry of Stanford University says that laughing 200 times will burn up the same amount of calories as 10 minutes on a rowing machine.

Does that make *Dumb and Dumber* a workout video?

Funny Bone

Your funny bone isn't actually a bone, it's a nerve—the ulnar nerve, in fact. This nerve is exposed as it travels over the medial condyle of the humerus, er, the bony knob at the end of your upper arm. Some clever (and unknown) medical student saw the punny resemblance between the words "humerus" and "humorous" and created the notion of the funny bone. Hitting your funny bone, however, is no laughing matter!

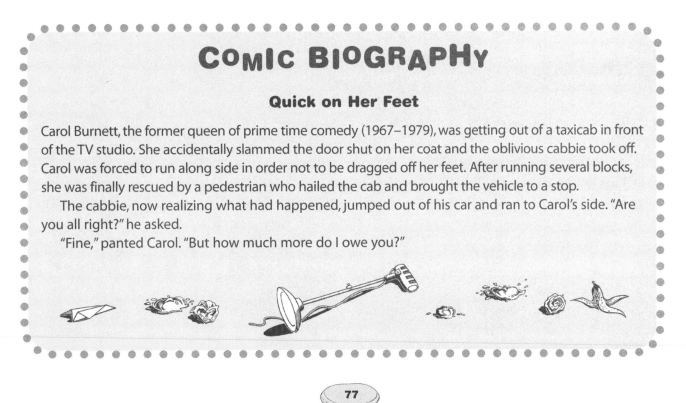

COMIC BIOGRAPHY

Quick on Her Feet

Carol Burnett, the former queen of prime time comedy (1967–1979), was getting out of a taxicab in front of the TV studio. She accidentally slammed the door shut on her coat and the oblivious cabbie took off. Carol was forced to run along side in order not to be dragged off her feet. After running several blocks, she was finally rescued by a pedestrian who hailed the cab and brought the vehicle to a stop.

The cabbie, now realizing what had happened, jumped out of his car and ran to Carol's side. "Are you all right?" he asked.

"Fine," panted Carol. "But how much more do I owe you?"

Tongue Twisters

Attempt to articulate these tricky tongue-tanglers quickly in triplicate.

Red leather, yellow leather.

Around the rugged rocks, the ragged rascal ran.

Rubber baby buggy-bumpers.

The sixth shiek's sixth sheep is sick.

The skunk sat on a stump, the skunk thunk the stump stunk, but the stump thunk the skunk stunk.

The clothes moth's mouth's closed.

She shall sell seashells.

How much wood would a woodchuck chuck if a woodchuck could chuck wood?

Bugs' black blood.

Eight apes ate eight apples.

Cool clean canned clams.

A stiff stack of thick steaks.

Toyboat, toyboat, toyboat.

In the Bag

A guy was trying to cross the border into the next country on his bicycle. Two suspicious-looking bags were tied to the back of the bike.

The border guards stopped him and said, "Hey, buddy, what's in the bags?"

"Sand," said the man.

The guards pulled off the two bags and examined them. They both contained only sand, just as the man said, so they waved him through the border.

This went on each week for six months. And each time the guards examined the bags they still found only sand.

One week the man stopped coming. One of the guards ran into the man downtown after work.

"Hey buddy," said the guard. "You sure had us going. We knew you were smuggling something."

The man just grinned.

"C'mon and tell me," whispered the guard. "I won't say anything. What were you smuggling?"

"Bicycles," said the man.

Burma-Shave: The Unknown Comic with an Edge

Years ago, when American families motored through the heartland on their way to a favorite vacation spot, they looked forward to reading the silly rhymes posted along the highways by the Burma-Shave company. Burma-Shave was a shaving cream for men, and the clever rhymes were posted—one line at a time—along highways and back roads all over the country. Kids and grownups tried to guess what the next rhyme would be before they drove past it. The highway poet remains anonymous, but here are a few of his, or her, best rhymes, broken up into separate lines as they appeared on separate signs along the way.

The whale
Put Jonah
Down the hatch
But coughed him up
Because he scratched.
Burma-Shave.

Does your husband
Misbehave
Grunt and rumble
Rant and rave?
Shoot the brute
Some Burma-Shave.

Ben
Met Anna
Made a hit
Neglected beard
Ben-Anna Split.
Burma-Shave.

The Nickname Game

Why do they call her Volleyball?
She's got plenty of bounce.

Why do they call him Birdseed?
He fits the bill.

JOKIN' AROUND

Goin' Bowling

The family went bowling one night and brought seven-year-old Stevie for the first time. Along with the rest of the family, Stevie laced up his bowling shoes and then went to select a ball. Everyone else chose one, but Stevie could not make up his mind.

Ten minutes went by and finally Father said, "Stevie, just pick a ball. We don't have all night."

"But I can't!" wailed Stevie. "Every ball I pick up has holes in it!"

Why do they call her Icecube?
She's so cool.

Why do they call him Ace?
He's such a card.

Why do they call her Strawberry?
She's good in a jam.

Why do they call him Needles?
He's so sharp.

Why do they call her Sunny?
She's so bright.

Why do they call him Fingers?
You can always count on him.

Why do they call her Sugar?
She's so refined.

Why do they call him Fleece?
He's always on the lam.

Why do they call him Buck?
He's got a lot of cents.

Why do they call you Mushroom?
Because I'm a fun guy!

Goofballs

Brother: How can you tell that elephants like to swim?
Sister: They always have their trunks on.

"Dad! There's a giant monster under my bed."
"Don't be silly. There's no such thing."
"Then how come I can touch the ceiling with my nose?"

Mother: Jimmy, your ear is bleeding!
Jimmy: I know, I accidentally bit it.
Mother: How could you bite your own ear?
Jimmy: I was standing on a chair.

Troy: Hey, what time does your new watch say?
Jimmy: It doesn't say anything. I have to look at it.
Troy: Don't be such a smart aleck!
Jimmy: Yeah? Well, what does yours say?
Troy: Tick, tick, tick, tick.

Why are the keys on this piano so yellow?
The elephant must have forgotten to brush.

Mother: You sent Jimmy down to the hardware store for some duct tape, right?
Father: Yes. But that was over an hour ago.
Mother: Well, he just phoned from the store and wants to know how big the duck is.

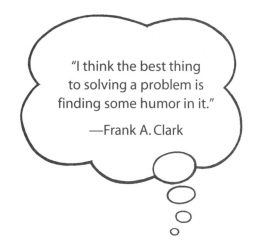

"I think the best thing to solving a problem is finding some humor in it."
—Frank A. Clark

Teacher: Does anyone know what it means to recycle?
Amy: That's when I have to ride my older sister's bicycle instead of getting a new one.

Store Manager: Ma'am, I've shown you every type of perfume we carry. Isn't there anything you'd like to buy?
Mother: Sorry, but your prices don't make any scents to me.

Troy: Our family just bought us one of those furry, Chinese dogs.
Jimmy: Chow?
Troy: No thanks, I just ate.

Jimmy: Well, our family bought one of those skinny greyhound types of dog.

Troy: Whippet?

Jimmy: Oh no! I only pet it.

Megan: I think our dog likes shopping.

Jason: How can you tell?

Megan: We just got back from the flea market, and he's itching to go back.

"I'm on the new seafood diet."
"Is it working?"
"Yeah, whenever I see food, I eat it!"

OOPS!

Draw a line to match each "OOPS!" to the proper picture.

OOPS! I'm stuck in the elevator door!

OOPS! My pigtails are too tight!

OOPS! I swallowed my spoon!

Jimmy: My mom says our kitchen floor is so clean we could eat off it.

Troy: Cool! At our house only the cat is allowed to do that!

"I hate that snobby Christina. Because of her I lost a hundred pounds."
"Wow! What did she do?"
"Stole my boyfriend."

"Doctor, my ear keeps ringing."
"You should get an unlisted ear."

What do you call a boomerang that doesn't come back?
A stick.

"Bugs give me the creeps!"
"What about spiders?"
"No way! I don't even like looking at them."
"Then it's a good thing you didn't see that one crawl into your shoe."

Trent: Hey, Jimmy, why didn't you stick around for the second act of the school play last night?

Jimmy: Because on the program it said "Two Years Later" and I had to be home by nine.

"Can I have a dollar for a sandwich?"

"If you like, but it probably won't taste very good."

Didja hear about the farmer who bought a farm a mile long and an inch wide?
He's raising spaghetti.

"This is the toughest sponge cake I ever ate."
"That's funny, the sponges I used were fresh."

The classroom was full of noisy and wild misbehaving students. The new teacher tried getting their attention, but the class continued to ignore him. Finally, in a last attempt to get the students to listen, the frustrated teacher shouted out: "Excuse me, people. But can anyone tell me what we use our ears for?" One boy remarked: "We mostly use our rears for sitting down on."

Karl: What was all that noise a moment ago?

Trent: That was me practicing my violin. Do you think I have a gift for playing?

Karl: No, but I'll give you one for stopping!

There's just one hard thing about parachute jumping.
The ground.

"She sure gave you a dirty look."
"Who?"
"Mother Nature."

Teacher: What does it mean when the barometer is falling?

Trent: It means whoever nailed it up didn't do a good job.

Megan: I think my mom must be the strongest person in the world.

Troy: Why do you say that?

Megan: Because everyday she picks up my entire room using only her bare hands.

Jimmy: Mom! Amy fell down the stairs!
Mother: Don't worry, honey. The doctor's taking steps to treat her.

"Will this road take me to Bakersville?"
"No, you'll have to drive there yourself."

Why did the weirdo throw the clock out the window?
Only a weirdo would throw a clock out the window!

Dad: Son, if you were out in the country, far from here, and only had a compass, how would you use it to find your way back?
Jimmy: Easy. I'd sell it for a few bucks and then buy a bus ticket home.

Troy: How much is that puppy?
Store Clerk: He's $50 or nothing.
Troy: Okay, I'll take him for nothing.

Neighbor: Young man, your cat was digging around in my garden!
Jimmy: I promise he'll never do that again.
Neighbor: How can you be so sure?
Jimmy: He was only burying your hamster he caught last night. But he's finished up by now.

"I can always tell when it's time for a snack."
"How?"
"My big hand is on the cookie jar and my little hand is inside."

When is it all right to belt a policeman?
When he gets in your car.

Megan: What kind of fish is that, Mister?
Pet Store Owner: Crappie.
Megan: Really? He looks fine to me.

Jimmy: We got a brand new roof and it didn't cost us a cent!
Megan: Why not?
Jimmy: The carpenters told us it was on the house.

Where's the best place to find cows?
At a moo-see-'em.

Teacher: You have to be the most annoying
          student I ever had!
Alex: Do I have to be?

"Can you help me? I'm looking for the bus
station."
"Is that thing lost again?!"

Father: Did you know the Anderson's dog can
          actually play video games?
Jimmy: He's not so smart. I played five games
          with him once, and he only won twice.

Two bank robbers were making their getaway
in a stolen car.
    "Turn around and see if the cops are
following us," said Joe.
    "But how can I tell if they're cops?" asked
Bill.
    "From their flashers," said Joe.
    "Okay." So Bill turned and looked out the
back window. "Yes, no, yes, no, yes, no . . ."

"Did you forget you were
supposed to call me last night?"
"I don't remember."

"My sister never helps clean up the downstairs
family room."
"Why not?"
"She says working in the basement is
beneath her."

Amy: What kind of jeans are those?
Rosie: Guess.
Amy: I have no idea.
Rosie: I told you: Guess.
Amy: I simply asked what kind they are.
Rosie: Guess! Guess!
Amy: You don't have to be rude about it!

"Mom! You know that red light you just drove
through? It's following us!"

Megan: Do you believe in ESP and seeing the
          future?
Wanda: Oh yes. In fact, my uncle had a
          terrible accident because he didn't
          pay attention to the signs.
Megan: Really?
Wanda: Yeah, especially the signs Stop and
          No Left Turn.

JOKIN' AROUND

From the Loopy Library

What do the following books have in common?

Blood Clots
The Hermit on the Hill
The Frozen Airplane Propeller
Wanda Always Stays Home

They never "circulate."

"The doctor said I should drink my medicine after a warm bath."
"And did you?"
"I'm not finished drinking the warm bath yet!"

"That cat just hissed at me!"
"Better watch out."
"But you told me your cat was friendly."
"It is, but that's not my cat."

Trent: Down at the bus stop, everyone is hunting for a few quarters some guy dropped.
Karl: I suppose you were looking around, too.
Trent: No, I was just standing there with my foot on the quarters.

Teacher: Do you believe in sharing, Alex?
Alex: Yes, ma'am.
Teacher: What's something you share with your brother?
Alex: Our parents.

"The doctor said I should take these pills on an empty stomach."
"That's right."
"But they keep getting stuck in my belly-button."

Mother: Jimmy, will you please sit up straighter?
Jimmy: If I sat up any straighter I'd be standing.

Watt's the Problem? (Light Bulb Jokes)

How many grandmothers does it take to change a light bulb?
Three. One to change it, one to powder it, and one to diaper it.

How many graduate students does it take to change a light bulb?
Ten. One to change the bulb and nine to write long, boring papers about it.

How many psychiatrists does it take to change a light bulb?
One. But the light bulb has really got to want to change.

How many wizards does it take to change a light bulb?
Depends on what you want the light bulb to change into.

How many undertakers does it take to change a light bulb?
None. They like their light bulbs dead.

How many seabirds does it take to change a light bulb?
About four or five terns ought to do the trick.

How many gangsters does it take to change a light bulb?
"Twelve. You gotta problem with that?"

How many Martians does it take to change a light bulb?
"What's a light bulb?"

How many cranky old men does it take to change a light bulb?
"Why change the light bulb? Everybody liked the old light bulb!"

Picto-Laugh #7

A pictograph is a very simple drawing of something funny. Can you guess what this little picto-laugh is showing? HINT: Think about a bug on wheels!

Anything for a Laugh

Teacher: Jimmy, I hope I didn't see you copying Amy's test paper.
Jimmy: Boy, I hope you didn't either!

Midge and Amy went to a county fair and found one of those old-fashioned fortune-telling weight machines. Amy got on first. When the card popped out, Midge read, "It says here that you are clever, beautiful, and charming." "Really?" said Amy. "Yeah," said Midge. "And it has your weight wrong, too."

Meghan: My mom complains about everything! She bought me two new T-shirts, a red one and a yellow one, and I put on the red one for school yesterday. At breakfast my mom says, "So what's wrong with the yellow one?"

Mother: Did you take a bath today?
Kyle: Why, is one missing?

Stranger: You catching any fish, kid?
Alex: Yes, sir! I caught at least twelve big ones.
Stranger: Do you know who I am? I'm the local fishing warden.
Alex: Do you know who *I* am? I'm the biggest liar in the county.

Mother: Your hair is starting to get wavy?
Father: Really?
Mother: Yes, it's waving goodbye!

Lisa: Whenever I'm down in the dumps, I get a new pair of shoes.
Midge: I thought that's where you got them.

Midge: I'm on a new diet and exercise program. Every morning after breakfast I go horseback riding.
Amy: Is it working?
Midge: So far the horse has lost ten pounds.

Melody: I think our neighbor Mrs. Johnson must be upset about something. She hasn't been over to visit for weeks.
Father: Find out what happened, and next time she comes over we'll try it again.

Larry: I've never had a problem with backseat driving, and I've been driving for over fifteen years.
Luna: What kind of car do you drive?
Larry: A hearse.

Thom: At my job I have a hundred men under me.
Kurt: Where do you work?
Thom: The cemetery.
Kurt: Well, at *my* job everyone looks up to me.
Thom: What do you do?
Kurt: I'm a kindergarten teacher.

Teacher: What is a light year?
Melody: A year with very little homework.

Rosie: What kind of fish are you frying?
Mother: Smelt.
Rosie: I sure can. But what kind of fish is it?

Doctor: Young man, you're going to need a flu shot.
Matt: Will it hurt?
Doctor: I'll be fine, but thanks for asking.

Jimmy: Where were you born?
Derek: On Rivers Avenue.
Jimmy: You're lucky you weren't run over by a bus!

Amy: The dog bit me in a very painful spot.
Rosie: Where'd he bite you?
Amy: In the backyard!

Gretchen: How does Old MacDonald spell "farm"?
Heather: E. I. E. I. O.

Troy: Excuse me, are you the head doctor here?
Doctor: No, I'm the foot doctor.

JOKIN' AROUND

Jiggy Geography

Parasites are people from Paris

Peruse are people from Peru

Maracas are people from Morocco

Canyons are people from Kenya

Goblets are people from Turkey

Teacher: Do you know what we call the person who delivers children?
Melody: She's called Mom. She delivers me to school, to my girlfriends' houses, to the mall, to soccer practice . . .

Trent: That sure is cool exercise equipment.
Matt: Thanks, I got it at the gym.
Trent: Did they have a sale?
Matt: No, they had a sign that said Free Weights.

Heather: You should see my new watch. It's rustproof, dustproof, shockproof, waterproof, and never needs batteries.
Gretchen: Cool, let's see it.
Heather: I lost it. So if you should see it, let me know!

Jimmy: My older brother Dave crashed his car into a tree going forty miles an hour.
Troy: Wow! I didn't know trees could move that fast!

Geo-Giggles

Here are the name of six states. Put them in the correct blanks to make three silly state riddles.
HINT: The pictures will give you a clue!

NEW JERSEY

TENNESSEE

DELAWARE

MARYLAND

ARKANSAS

IDAHO

What did
_____?
She wore her
_____!

What did
_____?
She saw what
_____!

What did
_____?
She hoed her
_____!

Elephant Jokes

No one knows how or why, but about 40 years ago elephant jokes stampeded onto the scene and became extremely popular. Here are a few samples of loopy, sometimes bizarre, pachyderm humor:

Can an elephant jump higher than a house?
Of course. Houses can't jump at all.

Why do elephants lie on their back?
They like to trip low-flying birds with their feet.

Why did the elephants quit their job at the factory? They were tired of working for peanuts.

What did Jane say when she saw the elephants coming over the hill?
"Here come the elephants!"

What did Tarzan say?
"Here come the grapes!" He was color blind.

What do you get when you cross an elephant with peanut butter?
A pachyderm that sticks to the roof of your mouth.

What's the difference between an elephant and a grape?
Grapes are purple.

Picto-Laugh #8

A pictograph is a very simple drawing of something funny. Can you guess what this little picto-laugh is showing? HINT: Think about broken elevators!

Two In One

You have to complete TWO puzzles to get the answer to this riddle:

Why did the elephant sit on the marshmallow?

1. First use a simple alphabet code (A=B, B=C, C=D, etc.) to figure out the first part of the answer.

S N   J D D O   E Q N L

_____

E Z K K H M F   H M S N   S G D

_____

2. Then connect the dots to find the second part of the answer.

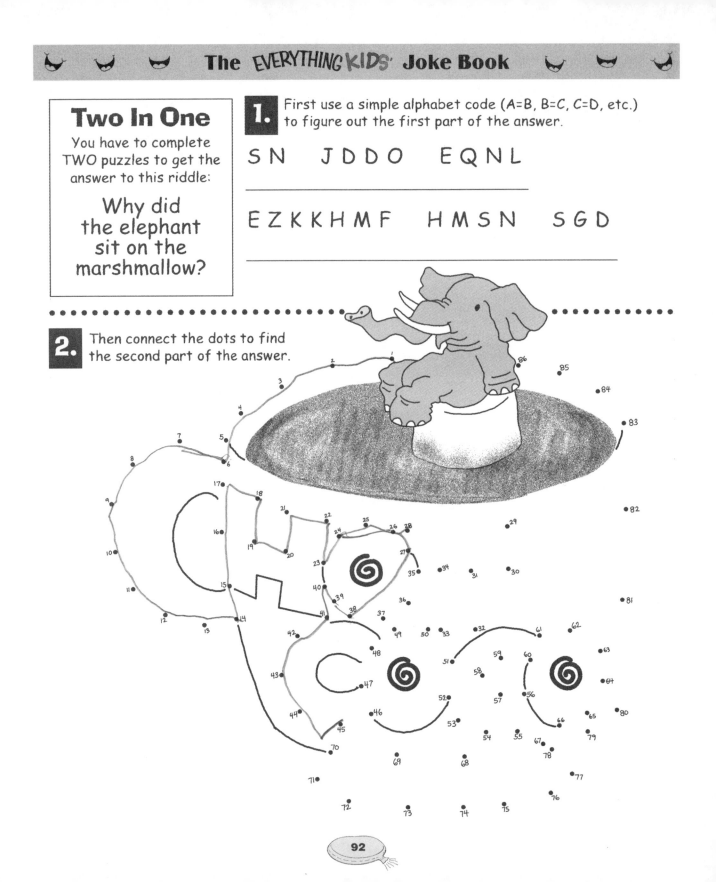

How do you get down off an elephant?
You don't get down off an elephant. You get down off a duck.

How do you catch an elephant?
Hide in the bushes and act like a peanut.

How do you get the wrinkles out of an elephant's skin?
Take him out of the dryer as soon as it stops.

Why don't elephants smoke?
Their butts are too big to set in the ashtrays.

Why are elephants easier to find in Alabama?
Because in Alabama you'll find Tuscaloosa (tusks are looser).

What weighs 2000 pounds, has big ears, tusks, and two trunks?
An elephant going on vacation.

What's big and gray and goes up and down, up and down?
An elephant bungee jumping.

Elemorphant

Can you turn an elephant into a peanut in three steps? Start with the word ELEPHANT. In each step, you can do only one of the following things—delete a group of letters, add a letter, or change one letter into another. Remember, you have to end up with PEANUT in Step 3! HINT: Keep track of the letters on the lines provided.

ELEPHANT

1. _____

2. _____

3. _____

Jay Leno was once asked to name a comedian's most important tool. "A tape recorder!" he replied. Not to record the comedian, but to record the audience. Leno urges new comedians to listen and relisten to their live performances and note when the audience laughed, when they didn't laugh, if the jokes were fast enough, loud enough, smart enough. Armed with this new information, a budding comedian can delete the bad jokes, sharpen up the better ones, and make the next gig even funnier.

Join the Laugh Riot Squad:
Anecdotes and Advice for Would-be Comedians

Be a Standup Comedian

Comedians are called **standup**s because they *stand up* in front of an audience and tell jokes. Most of them don't wear silly costumes or makeup, or use props or furniture. (A few do, but they are the exceptions.) Most comedians dress very simply. Their only prop is a microphone.

What audiences enjoy most about comedians is not how they look but how well they tell a joke or funny story. Everyone enjoys a good laugh, and comedians are experts in laughter.

▶ Speak clearly and loud enough to be heard. Don't mumble, but don't shout, either.

▶ Relax. Stand up straight and don't worry about what to do with your hands. Many comedians put their hands in the pockets of their pants or sport jacket.

▶ Don't laugh at your own jokes. It's your audience's job to laugh. It's your job to tell the joke with a straight face.

▶ After you tell your joke or funny story, give your audience time to laugh. Don't rush or speak too fast. Once the laughter starts to get quiet or dies down, then begin your next joke.

▶ Practice telling jokes into a mirror. If you can feel comfortable in front of your own reflection, you'll feel comfortable anywhere!

▶ Watch and listen to other comedians. You can learn a lot from observing the pros.

WORDS to KNOW

Monologue: the routine of a standup comic

Standup: comedians who stand up in front of their audiences and tell jokes

Routine: a comedian's collection of jokes that is done as an act over and over

Beat: a pause or break in the dialogue for comic effect

More Comedic Guidelines

1. When telling a joke or funny story, make sure you think it's funny.
2. If you are giving a speech or **monologue**, tell your funniest joke first.
3. Never begin with "Here's a joke," or "Now, this is funny . . ."
4. Know when to quit. Shakespeare said, "Brevity is the soul of wit." That means "Keep it short!"

Beats

As musicians know, keeping the beat is crucial. Comedians also keep the beat. A **beat** is a pause or break in dialogue. One-liners are spoken without a beat. But putting in a beat and knowing *where* to put it and *how long* to make it are the marks of an experienced comedian. Take the following line and add a beat:

> I'm a terrible cook. All the gingerbread boys I make are nearsighted. So I've started using contact raisins.

> I'm a terrible cook. All the gingerbread boys I make are nearsighted. (beat) So I've started using contact raisins.

Take just the right amount of time within the beat, and you end up with two jokes instead of one. Your audience will laugh after "nearsighted" and after "contact raisins."

Comedy expert Melvin Helitzer, who used to write for Sammy Davis, Jr., Shari Lewis, and Art Linkletter among others, advises would-be comedians that the average number of jokes in a comic monologue is 4 jokes per minute or 2 jokes plus 1 funny story.

That means in a five-minute standup **routine** you should have a supply of 20 jokes, or 7 funny stories, or a combo of both.

COMIC BIOGRAPHY

Glued to Their Seats:
A Lesson in Comic Timing

Eleonora Duse (1859–1924), an Italian megastar famous for making the audience weep at her over-the-top dramatic roles, was just as good at wowing the audiences in a good comedy. Take this story: She once got into a heated tiff with a young actress who thought that *she* was just as good as The Duse (as she was sometimes called).

"I can make the audience laugh at *me*," said the younger actress. "Even if you're onstage with me."

The Duse aimed to set the whippersnapper straight. "I can make the audience laugh and I can be *offstage*!"

The two women struck a bet. In their next show together, The Duse played a scene where she set down a glass of wine before exiting on a comic line. The next scene was the young actress's big moment in the show. Before her exit, however, The Duse set her glass down on a table, with half of the glass's bottom hanging over the edge!

During the young actress's scene, the audience paid no attention to her. Their attention was glued to The Duse's precarious wineglass, waiting for it to fall over at any moment. When the young actress realized what was going on, she became boiling mad. But she kept her cool. While she continued to play the scene, she strolled over to the wineglass and casually reached out to move it. But she couldn't. The Duse had applied glue to the bottom of the glass before the play began. So, throughout the rest of the young actress's scene she wrestled with the wineglass, trying to move it, sending the audience into fits of laughter—laughter set into motion by The Duse's perfect comic timing.

Tell the joke to individual friends or family members. You'll soon feel how long the beat needs to be in order to make it work. Only by telling (and listening) to lots of jokes told in lots of ways can you learn the secrets of comic timing.

Fresh A-peal: The Funniest Fruit

Slipping on a banana peel—that's the world's oldest joke, right? Most people would agree. And years ago, when moving pictures started cranking up, silent comedians slipped on thousands of banana peels in thousands of picture reels.

Leave it to Chaplin to make something old look new again. Charlie Chaplin (1889–1977) was a film and comic genius of the early 20th century. Besides making and starring in his own classics, he was always generous with advice and ideas for new directors and writers.

Once, a new screenwriter arrived in Hollywood and was having trouble with a scene involving the old banana peel gag. The writer asked Chaplin, "Charlie, what should I do? I'm at my wit's end. A prim and proper lady slipping on a banana peel has been done a million times. How do I make it funny?

"Should the camera show the banana first, then the lady walking? Or the lady walking, and then the peel? Or just the lady suddenly slipping? What do I do!"

Chaplin had the answer: "Have your camera show the lady walking. Then show the peel.

FUN FACT

Simon Says: Give Me a "K" Sound!

According to old-time funnyman Willie Clark in Neil Simon's popular play *The Sunshine Boys* (made into a film starring comedy veterans George Burns and Walter Matthau), words are funny if they have a K sound in them. Neil Simon even makes a list of the funniest words. See if you agree:

Chicken
Pickle
Cupcake
Cookie
Cucumber
Car keys
Cleveland

Come to think of it, a lot of words relating to comedy have the K sound: comic, crazy, kooky, cut-up, kick, wacky, cartoon, heckle, joke, quip, clown, prank, wisecrack, kidding, caper, cracking up, tricky, tickle, slapstick, shtick, skit, funky, screwy, quirky, flaky, freaky, chuckle, snicker, and yuk!

Then show the lady and the peel together. Then show the lady *stepping* over the peel."

"That's it?" asked the writer.

"Then," said Chaplin, "show the lady falling into a manhole!"

Besides slipping on their peels, comedians have made bananas the honorary pet fruit of funny business, the mascot of mayhem.

- **Going bananas** means someone is crazy.
- **Banana oil** is exaggerated talk or insincere flattery.
- A **banana** is a goofy person.
- Today throughout Great Britain, school kids call a weirdo a 'nana.
- Woody Allen wrote, directed, and starred in a hilarious hit called *Bananas* in 1971.

COMIC BIOGRAPHY

As Thousands Laugh

Neil Simon, by joke count alone, is the funniest man in America. He is the author of such comedy hits as *The Odd Couple*, *Plaza Suite*, *The Prisoner of Second Avenue*, *Biloxi Blues*, and *Laughter on the 23rd Floor*. He has written for television, films, and the stage and has won two Tonys and the Pulitzer Prize.

Averaging 2 to 3 jokes per page for a comedy script, Simon has written over 10,000 jokes—and counting!

That's a lot of punch lines.

WORDS to KNOW

Burlesque: A show of many skits with singing, dancing, and comedy

FUN FACT

Not Quite Himself

Did you know that Charlie Chaplin once entered a "Charlie Chaplin Look-alike Contest" held in Monaco and won third place?

> In the early 19th century, comedians performed in music halls and burlesque joints. The star comedian of the show was called the **top banana**, and next the **second banana**, and so on. Experts aren't exactly sure where the name comes from, but there are two theories. It might come from a famous sketch performed in **burlesque** halls that involved two clowns sharing a banana. Or it might refer to the stuffed, oversized (and sometimes water-filled!) bananas that early comics carried onstage to bonk each other over the head. These banana props were a version of the well-known slapstick.

comedies by Plautus and Aristophanes, a surefire audience-pleaser was any scene where a slave got to beat up his master. To make the scene even funnier, and to ensure the paying audience members sitting in the back row got their full enjoyment (there were

Slapstick

Watching two people pretend to wrestle and brawl has always struck other people as a laugh riot. As Will Rogers once said, "Everything is funny as long as it is happening to somebody else." In early Greek and Roman

WORDS to KNOW

Slapstick: 1. two wooden slats that are slapped together to make the sound of something striking something else; 2. silly, wild goofiness

World's Oldest Joke

The world's oldest written joke is written on a dried clay tablet over 3,000 years old! The tablet (along with more than 25,000 other tablets) was discovered by British archeologists in the 1850s as they unearthed the forgotten library of Ashurbanipal, king of ancient Assyria.

The tablet tells the humorous story of a boy being reprimanded by his father for not attending school. And like all good stories, it begins with a joke that reads, roughly translated:

Father: What are you doing?
Son: Nothing.
Father: Well, don't do it around here.

Although the clay tablets were collected for His Highness in the first millennium B.C., the stories that many of them tell are much older. Ashurbanipal's language (Sumerian) was spoken long before 2500 B.C., so who knows how old the joke *really* is!

no microphones or closed-circuit TVs in those days), the players used slapsticks. These were long wooden bats made of two slats that "slapped" together whenever the bat struck an object, like a master's noodle or his backside.

Comedians continued to use the noisy props up through the early part of the 20th century. Nowadays, the term **slapstick** refers to silly, knockabout, wild-and-crazy goofiness.

The Oldest Joke?

No one knows exactly who said the world's first joke or when, though it was probably a **sight gag:** Uglug the caveman ran into a mastodon or stepped in some dinosaur doo-doo while pursuing dinner, then watched his friends fall out of the trees with whoops of laughter. (The one friend who didn't fall out of the tree was the world's first critic.) By repeating his goof, practicing his timing, and

Sight gag: a joke that you need to see (like someone slipping on a banana peel) and usually has no words

WORDS to KNOW

Dilemma: a tough problem or sticky situation

FuN FACT

Dumb Instinct

When filming the hit comedy *Dumb and Dumber*, actor Jim Carrey changed the ending of the story. In the last scene, a busload of beautiful bikini models stop and ask for directions. The two dumb heroes, Harry and Lloyd, were supposed to board the bus, join the girls, and live happily ever after. But Carrey said that his character Lloyd was just too dumb to get on the bus. In fact, Carrey refused to act the scene as written; he would only let it be filmed with Lloyd and Harry walking away from the bus as it drives off.

Carrey proved to be right. The scene is much funnier! Lloyd (and Harry) are too stupid to realize they can join the pretty girls. The final scene of *Dumb and Dumber* is now a comedy classic. Carrey's lesson to all aspiring comedians? Trust your instincts!

packing up a portable supply of dino dung, Uglug might have performed his jokes for other villages and cave communities, thus creating the world's first road show.

According to the Jewish and Christian traditions, the first comic was actually God! In the second chapter of the book of Genesis, God creates the first man out of the clay, or dust, of the earth. The first man is named Adam. The Hebrew word for dirt or ground is *adamah*. In other words, the first guy was known as Dusty.

Don't believe it? O-pun up Genesis and read it.

De-Laughs in Dilemma

A **dilemma** is a tough problem or a sticky situation. Physical funny man Bill Irwin, featured on the "Don't Worry, Be Happy" video, once said that "The heart of clowning is how to get yourself into a dilemma." Once *in* a problem, an audience loves watching how a clown or comedian will get themselves *out*— whether it's Laurel and Hardy pushing a heavy piano up a long flight of stairs or Pee-Wee Herman doing his Big Shoe Dance to calm an angry motorcycle gang.

Rosie's Rule: "Mix It Up"

Rosie O'Donnell once gave a clue to comedy on the air. She explained to her television show audience how she teaches her son Parker the funny business: "Take two things that you normally don't see together, and *put* them together." Little kids begin with silly starters like, "Did you ever see a duck dancing? Did you ever see a pig drive a truck?" But Rosie's Rule applies to big kids, too. That's how comedians get ideas for gags and jokes. Notice all the successful comedies that follow the same rule:

Mix an overweight, nerdy professor and a sexy, handsome guy and you get:
The Nutty Professor

A loud, bossy Las Vegas lounge singer and a convent of quiet nuns:
Sister Act

A super-muscly, macho tough-guy and a classroom of 5-year olds:
Kindergarten Cop

A lawyer who always has to tell the truth:
Liar, Liar

Can't Do It!

The answer to each of these riddles is a compound word. Circle each answer as you find it in the letter grid, then write the word on the line next to each riddle. You get one hint!

What kind of pet can't go to the vet? _____ CARPET _____

What kind of key can't open a door? _____

What kind of pen can't write a letter? _____

What kind of bow can't be untied? _____

What kind of pot can't hold water? _____

What kind of toe can't be on your foot? _____

What kind of house can't get a new roof? _____

What kind of hand can't wear a ring? _____

What kind of drum can't play in a band? _____

What kind of bell can't be rung? _____

What kind of ship can't get wet? _____

What kind of crow can't fly? _____

```
B D Y D M K T S
A E M E T E I C
H W S A P Y M H
A N R R G B I O
N Y A D J O S L
D C I R A A T A
C R N U C R L R
U O B M K D E S
F W O N P U T H
F B W X O A O I
K A J J T I E P
G R P I G P E N
H O U S E F L Y
D U M B B E L L
G R M R F R M F
```

A Clue to Be Clueless

The late Steve Allen—comic, author, and television personality—said that most humor is based on confusion. "Some of the best jokes are the result of two people not understanding each other." For example, this gag:

Grandpa: My brand new hearing aid is the most expensive you can buy. It cost me over four thousand dollars.
Alex: What kind is it?
Grandpa: A quarter to four.

Another example of comic confusion occurs when people don't tell you everything at once:

Liz: Was I ever a dummy! I threw the baby's blanket out the window.
Shirley: I hope the baby doesn't catch pneumonia.
Liz: Oh, don't worry. The baby was still in the blanket.

Allen advises young comics to practice their joke-writing skills by seeing how many funny lines they can think up that would come after this sentence:

"Do you know where I can get a sandwich?"

Double Definitions

Sometimes the same word means different things to different people. In an interview, Tom Stoppard, the writer of *Rosencrantz and Guildenstern Are Dead* and *Shakespeare in Love*, was asked what his next play was about.

"It's about to make a lot of money," Stoppard replied.

HA,HA,HA!

HA, HA, HA!

HA, HA, HA!

How You Say. . .

Listen to Robin Williams in any of his films, or even in a TV interview. He uses a different voice or accent every other sentence. And when he's not talking, he's buzzing, hissing, booming, or creaking. We're not laughing at his words. We're laughing at his vocal expression. In other words, what can make a joke funny is not what you say, but *how* you say it.

When you tell a joke next time, use a different voice for each line. If there are different people (or animals) in your joke, give them each a unique way of speaking.

Need inspiration? Listen to Martin Short as the weird Franck Eggelhoffer in Steve Martin's *Father of the Bride*. Listen to Bronson Pinchot as he steals the scene in *Beverly Hills Cop* with his crazy accent. Then there's always the growling, shrieking Bobcat Goldthwait in the *Police Academy* movies, or his partner Michael Winslow who can make any sound in the known universe using just his mouth. There's the squawking Gilbert Godfrey and the demented Judy Tenuta, and the tight-lipped French Stewart on *Third Rock from the Sun* and grown-up Adam Sandler whining like a goofy little twerp.

Actors who are talented at creating different voices sometimes end up in animated films or TV cartoons. Next time you have a cartoon on the tube, check out the names listed under the heading "Voices." You may be surprised.

FUN FACT

Comic Relief

The first Comic Relief, a benefit to raise awareness and money for America's homeless, was televised on March 29, 1986. It was the first benefit featuring only comedians and was hosted by that great comic triple threat: Whoopi Goldberg, Robin Williams, and Billy Crystal. In the show's four and one-half hours jokesters from A to Z (Louis Anderson to Bob Zmuda) raised $2,500,000. That averages out to more than $9,000 per minute!

WORDS to KNOW

Straight man/Straight woman: the member of a comedy team who sets up the jokes and lets the gag player deliver the punch line

Going Straight for the Laughs

One of the most valuable players in a comedy team or a funny movie or television sitcom is the **straight man** or **straight woman**. The straight player seldom gets to say the big jokes or do the goofy stunts. The straight player sets up the jokes and lets the gag player deliver the punch line. The straight player stands calmly by and watches the other comic get wild and crazy. For instance, in a silly exchange like the following:

"I haven't slept for three days."
"Why not?"
"I only sleep at night."

The straight player is the one who says "Why not?"

COMIC BIOGRAPHY

Poor Marx for Comedy

Groucho Marx, the cigar-chewing, bushy-eyebrowed, crouch-walking leader of the nutty Marx Brothers, once confided to a director his surefire method for testing whether a joke was funny or not. Groucho would tell the joke to Zeppo, the quiet brother who played the romantic roles in their films. "If Zeppo likes it," said Groucho, "we throw it out!"

At first glance this may look like a boring, thankless chore. But an audience takes its cue from the straight player. When the straight man or woman laughs, gets angry, or reacts in just the right way to a joke, the audience will laugh *twice*—once at the joke and once at the straight player's reaction. The straight player makes the comic look even funnier.

Comedy teams always have one straight player. Dean Martin was the straight man to Jerry Lewis, Dan Rowan to Dick Martin, Oliver Hardy to Stan Laurel, David Spade to Chris Farley, and Gracie Allen to George Burns.

It takes talent and practice to be a comedian. It takes even more skill to play it straight!

Step on It! (Running Gags)

What is a **running gag**? It is a joke or funny stunt that happens several times throughout a single movie, scene, or TV show. A classic example is the poor Chihuahua that keeps getting sat on during *Airplane Two: The Sequel*. You never know when that pitiful pooch is going to turn up next, or who's going to sit on it.

Another hilarious example comes from Mel Brooks's *Young Frankenstein*. When we first meet the Frankenstein family's creepy housekeeper, Frau Blucher, the sound of her name alone is enough to frighten the horses. Even

FUN FACT

Famous Straight Men and Women

Gale Gordon in *The Lucy Show*
Richard Deacon in *The Dick Van Dyke Show*
Judd Hirsch in *Taxi*
Isabel Sanford in *The Jeffersons*
Dave Foley in *News Radio*
Mary Tyler Moore in *The Mary Tyler Moore Show*
David Spade in *Just Shoot Me*

WORDS to KNOW

Running gag: a joke or stunt that happens several times in a movie, play, TV show, or standup routine

WORDS to KNOW

Comic motion: actions that are funny, like someone climbing out of a swimming pool with all her clothes on.

toward the end of the movie, when someone deep in the castle's underground lab says "Frau Blucher," the horses' muffled braying can be heard in the courtyard far outside!

A running gag can be wordless, simply a physical stunt. A favorite running joke of movie fans is Inspector Clouseau's pal Kato in the *Pink Panther* comedies. The dimwitted

COMIC BIOGRAPHY

Getting His Feet Wet

Mack Sennett was one of old-time Hollywood's busiest comedy directors. Sennett had a big hand in creating the kooky Keystone Kops, Charlie Chaplin's Little Tramp character, and most of the films of Laurel and Hardy. Sennett also invented three major cliches of American comedy:

- A wacky chase scene (with cars, trains, motorcycles, etc.)
- A pie-throwing fight
- A beautiful girl loved by the crazy comedian

After Sennett became famous, a pesky young actor asked him what it took to be a good comedian. "You have to understand **comic motion**," explained Sennett.

"That's simple," said the fellow. "You mean like making funny faces?"

Suddenly, Sennett pushed the actor into a nearby swimming pool. When the wet and gasping fellow climbed out, Sennett said, "*That's* comic motion."

COMIC BIOGRAPHY

What a Ball!

Lucille Ball was the Queen of Comedy. Known for her zany physical humor, goofball costumes, and trademark flaming red hair and "ambulance-siren" wail, she starred in the number one TV show of the 1950s. Lucy was also one of the hardest working comedians on stage, TV, and films. Look at her output (and that doesn't even include the countless hours she spent rehearsing her perfectly timed comic shtick, songs, and dance routines):

124 radio episodes of *My Favorite Husband*
179 TV episodes of *I Love Lucy*
13 original *Lucy-Desi Comedy Hour* programs
156 episodes of *The Lucy Show*
149 episodes of *Here's Lucy*
and 79 movies!

Inspector has ordered Kato to attack him at any time without warning, day or night. Clouseau thinks that this will help keep him alert, on his toes, and sharpen his skills as a supersleuth. Throughout the films then, Kato will suddenly appear from nowhere, leap at the Inspector, and start a huge knockdown battle royale.

The TV comedy *Seinfeld* was full of running gags. A gag at the beginning of the show will turn up unexpectedly in the middle of the story or right before the closing credits.

Other running gags to watch for:

The woman with her pet dogs in *A Fish Called Wanda*.
The literal "running" gag of the jogging Buster Keaton in *A Funny Thing Happened On the Way to the Forum*.
The rubber hand with the ring (and the word "Munson") in *Kingpin*.
The plate glass window in *What's Up, Doc?*
The mysterious apartment in *The Ladies' Man*.
All of Ferris's well-wishers in *Ferris Bueller's Day Off*.

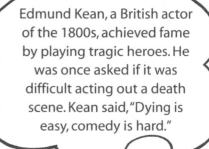

Edmund Kean, a British actor of the 1800s, achieved fame by playing tragic heroes. He was once asked if it was difficult acting out a death scene. Kean said, "Dying is easy, comedy is hard."

Carry a Big Shtick

A **shtick** is a collection of gimmicks or gags that a comedian relies on. Shtick comes from a Yiddish word meaning "bits and pieces" and was used to describe a small part in a play. The word now refers to the bits and pieces that make up a comedian's toolbox of verbal and physical humor.

Examples of comedians' shtick:

WORDS to KNOW

Shtick: the regular bits and pieces that make up a comedian's toolbox

Robin Williams: funny voices, improvisation, and quick changes of pace
Jim Carrey: wild facial expressions and exaggerated physical movements
Roseanne: weary, no-nonsense, suburban mother
Bill Murray: smarmy, "thinks he's cool" know-it-all
Adam Sandler: goofy, class clown
Jerry Lewis: wide-eyed, well-meaning bumbler

A Shtick List

Shtick can also refer to a widely used gimmick that never fails to provoke laughter. The oldest of these would be getting a pie thrown in your face or slipping on a banana peel. Other shtick include:

- Wearing clothes that are too big or too small
- Not paying attention while walking or riding a bicycle and bumping into a wall, door, or another person
- Someone asks you a question when your mouth is full
- Dressing up as the opposite sex in order to avoid someone
- Carefully reaching for a single item at a store but accidentally spilling hundreds all over the floor
- Getting a tie stuck in anything, especially in your food, a suitcase, or a closing elevator door
- During a conversation, just as you are about to say an important word or phrase, a loud noise occurs (airplane, construction work, traffic, etc.)
- Sitting down at precisely the same time as someone else, or turning the page of a book at the same time
- Two frightened guys looking at each other and screaming

The Spit-Take

Try this well-used shtick: A friend says something shocking just as you are taking a sip of water. Your reaction? A sputtering blast of liquid all over you and your companion. This particular shtick is known as the **spit-take**, a time-honored method of getting a laugh.

WORDS to KNOW

Spit-take: when someone sprays a mouthful of liquid all over someone else in response to something said

Exit Laughing

"Nobody ever died of laughter," exclaimed Sir Max Beerbohm (1872–1956), a British caricaturist and wit. But Max was wrong. According to historians, there are at least two cases of hilarity producing fatal results. These two men both died from laughing too hard:

Thomas Urquhart, a Scottish writer and translator, in 1660
Calchas, a Greek fortuneteller, sometime before 800 B.C.

It's a good thing the jokes they heard are not on record!

Gen-X author David Foster Wallace uses the idea of deadly laughs for his monumental (1,079 pages!) bestseller *Infinite Jest*. In Wallace's book, the mysterious bad guys televise a movie called *Infinite Jest* that is so amusing, so entertaining, that people who watch it forget to sleep, eat, or drink and eventually starve to death!

The spit-take has been used on almost every TV sitcom and in countless films. It is also used in plays and comedy clubs (front row ticketholders beware!). But it's not the easiest joke to master. Timing is everything. The joke that provokes the spit-take must be heard clearly before the reaction takes place. And if the spit is too short or too long, the laughter turns into a groan.

Whenever you hear a joke, your reaction is a *take*. (In other words, how did you "take" the joke? Did you think it was silly, boring, stupid?) Comedians are experts at "doing a take" and can whip up laughter by simply reacting to the wild antics taking place around them. Many comedians do a take by looking directly into the camera or at the audience. It's as if they are saying, "Do you think this stuff is as ridiculous as I do?"

One word of caution: Be careful what you are drinking when you do a spit-take. After all, milk and grape juice can stain, and hot coffee might lead to an argument. The pros use cold water and avoid getting into "hot water!"

The Sight Gag

A sight gag is a joke without words. It does not mean wearing silly clothes or making a goofy grin. A sight gag is a well-planned joke that makes us laugh because of something we see, rather than something we hear.

Do You See What I See?

Can you find the 20 silly substitutions in this picture?

A classic example takes place in Jacques Tati's *Mr. Hulot's Holiday*. At a summer hotel, a group of strangers is playing cards. There are two tables, each with their own game. The roomful of serious players stare at the cards in their hands, oblivious to their surroundings. Mr. Hulot comes onto the scene looking for a missing ping-pong ball. As he bumbles around searching for his ball, Mr. H. nudges Mr. Gonzales, one of the card players who is sitting in a swivel chair. The chair rotates smoothly just as Mr. Gonzales, his nose buried in his hand, lays down a card. The card lands on the table *next to him* instead of his own table. Then Mr. H. swivels the chair back into place. The wrongly played card provokes a riot at both tables.

The scene is just as hilarious if you watch it with the sound turned off.

Here's another sight gag: A boy and girl are sitting at a coffee shop. She is drinking coffee, he is chewing bubble gum. The couple stops talking, stare meaningfully at each other, and then kiss. When the long, romantic kiss is over, suddenly it's the girl who blows a bubble.

Movies that are not strictly comedies may also contain sight gags. Look for the lovebirds in Melanie Daniels's speeding sports car in Hitchcock's *The Birds*. The sight gag adds just the right touch of humor to an otherwise nerve-wracking film.

Hunting for more ideas to create your own sight gags? Watch the amazing Mr. Bean, Roadrunner cartoons, *I Love Lucy* reruns, silent movies, or Mel Brooks's modern *Silent Movie*. *Ace Ventura, Pet Detective*; *Men in Black*; *Ghostbusters*; *Addams Family Values*; and every episode of *The Simpsons* contain loads of sight gags.

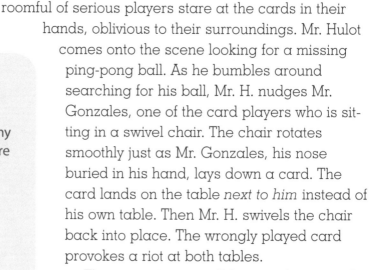

FUN FACT

Just Four Laughs

Only four comedies have won the Academy Award for Best Movie since the Oscars were first handed out in 1929:

It Happened One Night (1934)
You Can't Take It With You (1938)
The Apartment (1960)
Annie Hall (1977)

HA, HA, HA!
HA, HA, HA!
HA, HA, HA!

Young Frankenstein is a sight gag encyclopedia:

The girl flying through the window
The corpse's arm on the broken wagon
Igor's head on the laboratory shelf
The hermit spilling hot soup
The light from the unlit candelabra
The revolving bookcase

Parody

A **parody**, also known as a spoof or a takeoff, is a humorous imitation of something serious. Austin Powers is a parody of James Bond. *Airplane!* is a takeoff of *Airport*. Mel Brooks, a spoof specialist, created a hit parade of parodies: westerns (*Blazing Saddles*), monster movies (*Young Frankenstein*), and Hitchcock suspense films (*High Anxiety*).

WORDS to KNOW

Parody: a humorous imitation of something serious

Funny Playwright

George S. Kaufman wrote some of the funniest plays ever produced in America, including *The Man Who Came to Dinner* and *You Can't Take It With You*. He also wrote this punfully apt inscription for his gravestone:

Over My Dead Body

His friend Dorothy Parker got in the act and wrote one for herself:

Excuse My Dust

The best parodies are when the audience knows exactly what is being spoofed. Here's an example:

Mary had a little lamb
She tied him to the heater,
And everytime he turned around
He burned his little seater.

And another:

'Twas the hour before midnight
And all through the gloom
Not a creature was stirring,
Except in the tomb!

A Humor Quiz

What's the Punch Line?

Do you have what it takes to be a comedy writer? Test your H.Q. (Humor Quotient) by matching your answers against the standard joke lines. If you come up with lines that are even funnier (and make your friends and family chuckle), you should be writing for TV!

WORDS to KNOW

Punch line: the part of the joke that gets the laugh

1. Why did the weirdo throw the clock out the window?
   He wanted to see _____ _____.

2. *Mother:* Honey, I can't get the car started! I think it's flooded.
   Father: Where is it?
   Mother: In the _____ _____.

3. "Mom, I'm feeling upside down."
   "Upside down? What do you mean?"
   "Well, my nose _____ and my feet _____!"

4. My dad solved the parking problem: He bought a _____
   _____.

5. A fellow forgot to buy cheese for his mousetrap. So he cut out a magazine picture of a slice of cheese and put that in the trap instead. Amazingly enough, the trap worked. The next morning he went to inspect the trap and found what?

6. What's the best way to drive a baby buggy?

   _____ *its* _____.

7. "Doctor, will I be able to play the piano once the operation is over?"
   "Certainly."
   "That's funny, because _____."

8. A customer walks into a seafood restaurant and demands, "Do you serve crabs in this dump?"
   And the headwaiter replies, "_____."

9. *Jimmy:* What kind of dog is that?
   Troy: He's a police dog.
   Jimmy: He doesn't look like a police dog to me.
   Troy: Of course not.
   That's because he's _____ _____.

10. What does a 400-pound canary say?
    "_____."

11. Didja hear about the vampire that had a bad cold?
    His _____ *kept him up all night.*

12. What did the jogger say when he ran into the doctor's office?
    "_____!"

13. What does a baseball player do when his eyesight goes bad?
    He gets a job as _____.

14. *Customer:* Waiter, what is this fly doing in my soup?
    Waiter: _____.

15. "I see your son drives his own car now."
    "Yes, finally!"
    "How long did it take him to learn?"
    "About two-and-a-half _____."

16. "What are you going to give your little brother for Christmas this year?"
    "I haven't decided yet."
    "What did you give him last year?"
    "The _____."

17. "My Dad thinks he's a poodle."
    "Wow! How long has he thought that?"
    "Ever since he _____."

18. What did the baby mouse say to his mother the first time he saw a bat flying overhead?
    "Look, Mom, it's _____!"

19. What do you call a cat who likes lemonade?
    A _____ _____.

20. "Is that little kid your brother?"
    "He sure is."
    "He's awful short."
    "That's because he's my _____ _____."

Answers

1. *Time fly.*
2. Swimming pool.
3. Runs, smell.
4. Parked car.
5. A picture of a mouse, or rat.
6. *Tickle its feet.*
7. "I never could before."
8. "We serve anyone. Sit down!"
9. Undercover, or in disguise, or in the Secret Service.
10. "Here, kitty, kitty, kitty."
11. *Coffin.*
12. "*Ouch!*"
13. *An umpire.*
14. "The backstroke," or "the breast stroke," or "The dog paddle."
15. *Cars.*
16. Flu, measles, or whooping cough.
17. *Was a puppy.*
18. "*Superman!*" or "*an angel!*"
19. *Sour puss.*
20. Half brother.

Your H.Q. (Humor Quotient)

Right answers:

0–3: Bet you're a hit at family reunions.
4–8: Class Clown!
9–14: Hire a talent agent.
15 or more: Call Jim Carrey! He needs you on the set NOW!

Glossary

Beat: pause or break in the dialogue for comic effect

Burlesque: A show of many skits with singing, dancing, and comedy

Comic Motion: actions that are funny, like someone climbing out of a swimming pool with all her clothes on

Dilemma: a tough problem or sticky situation

Gag: a laugh-provoking remark, trick, or prank

Limerick: a light or humorous verse with a specific rhythm and rhyme scheme

Limick: a shortened version of a limerick

Monologue: the routine of a standup comic

One-liner: a joke that is told in one line or sentence

Parody: a humorous imitation of something serious

Pun: the humorous use of a word in such a way as to suggest two or more of its meanings or the meaning of another word with a similar sound

Punch line: the part of the joke that gets the laugh

Routine: a comedian's collection of jokes that is done as an act over and over

Running gag: a joke or stunt that happens several times in a movie, play, TV show, or standup routine

Shtick: the regular bits and pieces that make up a comedian's toolbox

Sight gag: a joke that you need to see (like someone slipping on a banana peel) and usually has no words

Slapstick: 1. two wooden slats that are slapped together to make the sound of something striking something else; 2. silly, wild goofiness

Spit-take: when someone sprays a mouthful of liquid all over someone else in response to something said

Spoonerism: a phrase where the first letters of a word are exchanged for another

Standup: comedians who stand up in front of their audiences and tell jokes

Straight man/Straight woman: the member of a comedy team who sets up the jokes and lets the gag player deliver the punch line

Puzzle Answers

page 3 • Hole In One

What did the witch use to
fix her broken jack-o'-lantern?

1. P_UPPY
2. J_U_MP
3. LU_M_MP
4. HAP_P_Y
5. SHAR_K_
6. SM_I_LE
7. SA_N_D
8. SLOP_P_Y
9. S_A_D
10. _T_UNA
11. _C_HURCH
12. C_H_INA

She used a

page 7 • Why Oh Why?

Why did the chicken cross the playground?

TO	GET	TO	THE	OTHER	SLIDE

Write the answer here.

page 12 • Picto-Laugh #1

a spider walking
across a mirror

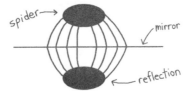

page 13 • Say What?

T		A	U		T		F	I	N	H
HE	O	W	T	S	N	A	R	Y	I	SG
HE		WAS			TRY			I		NG
	TO		TUNA			FISH				

Puzzle Answers

page 19 • Sounds Funny To Me

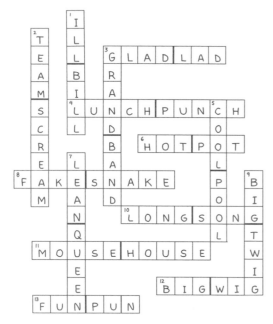

#5 a centipede with a wooden leg

#6 a watch dog

#2 a laughing farmer

#4 someone laughing their head off

#3 someone eating alphabet soup

a bee flying backwards #1

page 25 • Hink Pink Kriss Kross

³GLADLAD

⁴LUNCHPUNCH

⁶HOTPOT

⁸FAKESNAKE

¹⁰LONGSONG

¹¹MOUSEHOUSE

¹²BIGWIG

¹³FUNPUN

Down:
¹ILLBILL
²TEAMSCREME
⁵CHOOLPOLL
⁷LANDQUEE
⁹BIGTWIN
FMANQ
MEEE

page 31 • Picto-Laugh #2

a turtle on a skateboard

turtle pulled all the way into shell

page 48 • It's Rhyme Time

B U Y   FR Y

D Y E   E YE

PI E   WH Y

T R Y   C RY

There was a young boy who asked," Why Can't I look in my ear with my eye ? If I put my mind to it, I'm sure I could do it, But I'll never know till I try !"

page 49 • Bye Bye

I
C U
L 8 R

I see you later!

126

Puzzle Answers

page 52 • Picto-Laugh #3

aerial view of a person in a sombrero riding a bike without using their hands

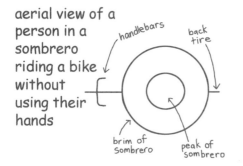

handlebars

back tire

brim of sombrero

peak of sombrero

page 53 • Love to Laugh

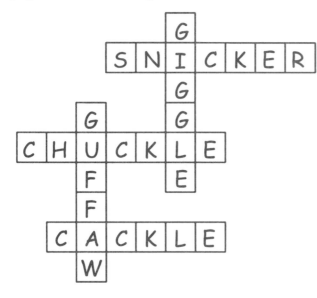

```
      G
S N I C K E R
      G
      G
  G   L
C H U C K L E
  F   E
  F
C A C K L E
  W
```

page 54 • Picto-Laugh #4

aerial view of a person in a sombrero frying an egg in a pan

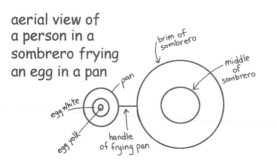

brim of sombrero

middle of sombrero

pan

egg white

egg yolk

handle of frying pan

page 55 • It's Joke Time!

What time is it when five tigers are chasing you?

What time is it when you have a toothache?

What time is it when baseball teams have a tie score?

What time is the same backward or forward?

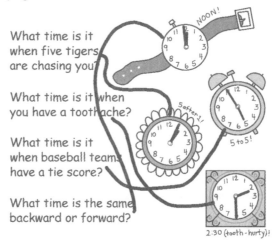

NOON!

5 after 1!

5 to 5!

2:30 (tooth-hurty)!

page 59 • Picto-Laugh #5

the blower of the world's biggest bubble gum bubble

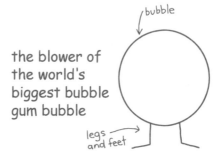

bubble

legs and feet

page 60 • Fill Me In

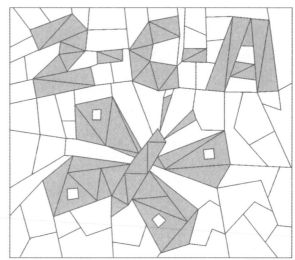

Puzzle Answers

page 66 • **Picto-Laugh #6**

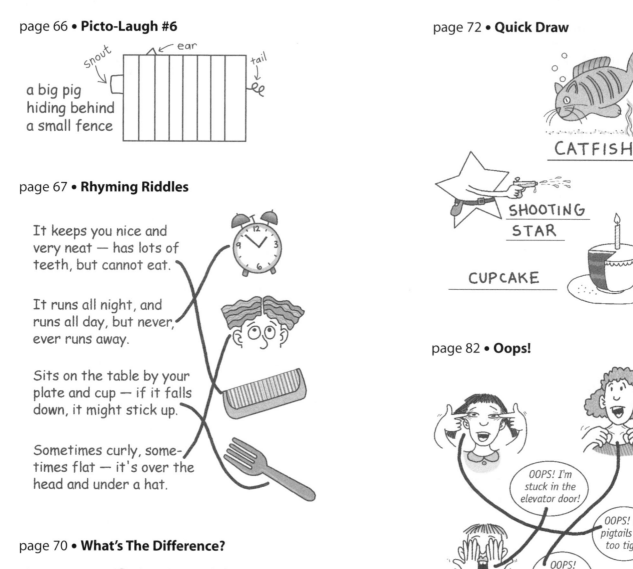

a big pig hiding behind a small fence

page 67 • **Rhyming Riddles**

It keeps you nice and very neat — has lots of teeth, but cannot eat.

It runs all night, and runs all day, but never, ever runs away.

Sits on the table by your plate and cup — if it falls down, it might stick up.

Sometimes curly, sometimes flat — it's over the head and under a hat.

page 70 • **What's The Difference?**

1. One CATCHES DROPS, and the other DROPS CATCHES.

2. One is BAD MONEY, and the other is a MAD BUNNY.

3. One WATCHES CELLS, and the other SELLS WATCHES.

4. One is an EASY CHEATER, and the other is a CHEESY EATER.

5. One is a BAD SALAD, and the other is a SAD BALLAD.

6. One is a FIT BUNNY, and the other is only a BIT FUNNY.

page 72 • **Quick Draw**

CATFISH

SHOOTING STAR

CUPCAKE

page 82 • **Oops!**

OOPS! I'm stuck in the elevator door!

OOPS! My pigtails are too tight!

OOPS! I swallowed my spoon!

Puzzle Answers

page 87 • Picto-Laugh #7

a boa constrictor that has just swallowed a Volkswagon Beetle

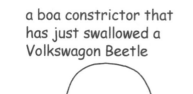

page 92 • Two-In-One

SN JDDO EQNL
TO KEEP FROM

EZKKHMF HMSN SGD...
FALLING INTO THE

page 90 • Geo-Giggles

What did

DELAWARE *(Dela wear)* ?

She wore her

NEW JERSEY !

What did

TENNESSEE *(Tennes see)* ?

She saw what

ARKANSAS *(Arkan saw)* !

What did

IDAHO *(Ida hoe)* ?

She hoed her

MARYLAND *(merry land)* !

page 91 • Picto-Laugh #8

a snake going up a flight of stairs

page 93 • Elemorphant

ELEPHANT

1. ~~ELE~~PHANT   delete ELE
2. P^EHANT   change H to E
3. PEAN^UT   add U

ELEPHANT

1. ELEPHAN^UT   add U
2. ELEP^EHANUT   change H to E
3. ~~ELE~~PEANUT   delete ELE

Puzzle Answers

page 105 • Can't Do It!

What kind of pet can't go to the vet? __CARPET__

What kind of key can't open a door? __KEYBOARD__

What kind of pen can't write a letter? __PIGPEN__

What kind of bow can't be untied? __RAINBOW__

What kind of pot can't hold water? __JACKPOT__

What kind of toe can't be on your foot? __MISTLETOE__

What kind of house can't get a new roof? __HOUSEFLY__

What kind of hand can't wear a ring? __HANDCUFF__

What kind of drum can't play in a band? __EARDRUM__

What kind of bell can't be rung? __DUMBBELL__

What kind of ship can't get wet? __SCHOLARSHIP__

What kind of crow can't fly? __CROWBAR__

```
B D Y D M K T S
A E M E T E I C
H W S A P Y M H
A N Y R R G B O
N Y A R G J B L
D C I R U J A A
C R N D M C O R
U O B U K A R S
F W O M P D L H
F B W N U T E I
K A X O A O P
G R J J T I E
  P I G P E N
H O U S E F L Y
D U M B B E L L
G R M R F R M F
```

page 115 • Do You See What I See?

Index

We Have EVERYTHING!

Everything® **After College Book**
$12.95, 1-55850-847-3

Everything® **Angels Book**
$12.95, 1-58062-398-0

Everything® **Astrology Book**
$12.95, 1-58062-062-0

Everything® **Baby Names Book**
$12.95, 1-55850-655-1

Everything® **Baby Shower Book**
$12.95, 1-58062-305-0

Everything® **Baby's First Food Book**
$12.95, 1-58062-512-6

Everything® **Barbeque Cookbook**
$12.95, 1-58062-316-6

Everything® **Bartender's Book**
$9.95, 1-55850-536-9

Everything® **Bedtime Story Book**
$12.95, 1-58062-147-3

Everything® **Bicycle Book**
$12.00, 1-55850-706-X

Everything® **Build Your Own Home Page**
$12.95, 1-58062-339-5

Everything® **Business Planning Book**
$12.95, 1-58062-491-X

Everything® **Casino Gambling Book**
$12.95, 1-55850-762-0

Everything® **Cat Book**
$12.95, 1-55850-710-8

Everything® **Chocolate Cookbook**
$12.95, 1-58062-405-7

Everything® **Christmas Book**
$15.00, 1-55850-697-7

Everything® **Civil War Book**
$12.95, 1-58062-366-2

Everything® **College Survival Book**
$12.95, 1-55850-720-5

Everything® **Computer Book**
$12.95, 1-58062-401-4

Everything® **Cookbook**
$14.95, 1-58062-400-6

Everything® **Cover Letter Book**
$12.95, 1-58062-312-3

Everything® **Crossword and Puzzle Book**
$12.95, 1-55850-764-7

Everything® **Dating Book**
$12.95, 1-58062-185-6

Everything® **Dessert Book**
$12.95, 1-55850-717-5

Everything® **Dog Book**
$12.95, 1-58062-144-9

Everything® **Dreams Book**
$12.95, 1-55850-806-6

Everything® **Etiquette Book**
$12.95, 1-55850-807-4

Everything® **Family Tree Book**
$12.95, 1-55850-763-9

Everything® **Fly-Fishing Book**
$12.95, 1-58062-148-1

Everything® **Games Book**
$12.95, 1-55850-643-8

Everything® **Get-A-Job Book**
$12.95, 1-58062-223-2

Everything® **Get Published Book**
$12.95, 1-58062-315-8

Everything® **Get Ready for Baby Book**
$12.95, 1-55850-844-9

Everything® **Golf Book**
$12.95, 1-55850-814-7

Everything® **Guide to Las Vegas**
$12.95, 1-58062-438-3

Everything® **Guide to New York City**
$12.95, 1-58062-314-X

Everything® **Guide to Walt Disney World®, Universal Studios®, and Greater Orlando, 2nd Edition**
$12.95, 1-58062-404-9

Everything® **Guide to Washington D.C.**
$12.95, 1-58062-313-1

Everything® **Herbal Remedies Book**
$12.95, 1-58062-331-X

Everything® **Home-Based Business Book**
$12.95, 1-58062-364-6

Everything® **Homebuying Book**
$12.95, 1-58062-074-4

Everything® **Homeselling Book**
$12.95, 1-58062-304-2

Everything® **Home Improvement Book**
$12.95, 1-55850-718-3

Everything® **Hot Careers Book**
$12.95, 1-58062-486-3

Everything® **Internet Book**
$12.95, 1-58062-073-6

Everything® **Investing Book**
$12.95, 1-58062-149-X

Everything® **Jewish Wedding Book**
$12.95, 1-55850-801-5

Everything® **Job Interviews Book**
$12.95, 1-58062-493-6

Everything® **Lawn Care Book**
$12.95, 1-58062-487-1

Everything® **Leadership Book**
$12.95, 1-58062-513-4

Everything® **Low-Fat High-Flavor Cookbook**
$12.95, 1-55850-802-3

Everything® **Magic Book**
$12.95, 1-58062-418-9

Everything® **Microsoft® Word 2000 Book**
$12.95, 1-58062-306-9

Available wherever books are sold!

Everything® **Money Book**
$12.95, 1-58062-145-7

Everything® **Mother Goose Book**
$12.95, 1-58062-490-1

Everything® **Mutual Funds Book**
$12.95, 1-58062-419-7

Everything® **One-Pot Cookbook**
$12.95, 1-58062-186-4

Everything® **Online Business Book**
$12.95, 1-58062-320-4

Everything® **Online Genealogy Book**
$12.95, 1-58062-402-2

Everything® **Online Investing Book**
$12.95, 1-58062-338-7

Everything® **Online Job Search Book**
$12.95, 1-58062-365-4

Everything® **Pasta Book**
$12.95, 1-55850-719-1

Everything® **Pregnancy Book**
$12.95, 1-58062-146-5

Everything® **Pregnancy Organizer**
$15.00, 1-58062-336-0

Everything® **Quick Meals Cookbook**
$12.95, 1-58062-488-X

Everything® **Resume Book**
$12.95, 1-58062-311-5

Everything® **Sailing Book**
$12.95, 1-58062-187-2

Everything® **Selling Book**
$12.95, 1-58062-319-0

Everything® **Study Book**
$12.95, 1-55850-615-2

Everything® **Tall Tales, Legends, and Outrageous Lies Book**
$12.95, 1-58062-514-2

Everything® **Tarot Book**
$12.95, 1-58062-191-0

Everything® **Time Management Book**
$12.95, 1-58062-492-8

Everything® **Toasts Book**
$12.95, 1-58062-189-9

Everything® **Total Fitness Book**
$12.95, 1-58062-318-2

Everything® **Trivia Book**
$12.95, 1-58062-143-0

Everything® **Tropical Fish Book**
$12.95, 1-58062-343-3

Everything® **Vitamins, Minerals, and Nutritional Supplements Book**
$12.95, 1-58062-496-0

Everything® **Wedding Book, 2nd Edition**
$12.95, 1-58062-190-2

Everything® **Wedding Checklist**
$7.95, 1-58062-456-1

Everything® **Wedding Etiquette Book**
$7.95, 1-58062-454-5

Everything® **Wedding Organizer**
$15.00, 1-55850-828-7

Everything® **Wedding Shower Book**
$7.95, 1-58062-188-0

Everything® **Wedding Vows Book**
$7.95, 1-58062-455-3

Everything® **Wine Book**
$12.95, 1-55850-808-2

Everything® **Angels Mini Book**
$4.95, 1-58062-387-5

Everything® **Astrology Mini Book**
$4.95, 1-58062-385-9

Everything® **Baby Names Mini Book**
$4.95, 1-58062-391-3

Everything® **Bedtime Story Mini Book**
$4.95, 1-58062-390-5

Everything® **Dreams Mini Book**
$4.95, 1-58062-386-7

Everything® **Etiquette Mini Book**
$4.95, 1-58062-499-5

Everything® **Get Ready for Baby Mini Book**
$4.95, 1-58062-389-1

Everything® **Golf Mini Book**
$4.95, 1-58062-500-2

Everything® **Love Spells Mini Book**
$4.95, 1-58062-388-3

Everything® **Pregnancy Mini Book**
$4.95, 1-58062-392-1

Everything® **TV & Movie Trivia Mini Book**
$4.95, 1-58062-497-9

Everything® **Wine Mini Book**
$4.95, 1-58062-498-7

Everything® **Kids' Baseball Book**
$9.95, 1-58062-489-8

Everything® **Kids' Joke Book**
$9.95, 1-58062-495-2

Everything® **Kids' Money Book**
$9.95, 1-58062-322-0

Everything® **Kids' Nature Book**
$9.95, 1-58062-321-2

Everything® **Kids' Online Book**
$9.95, 1-58062-394-8

Everything® **Kids' Puzzle Book**
$9.95, 1-58062-323-9

Everything® **Kids' Space Book**
$9.95, 1-58062-395-6

Everything® **Kids' Witches and Wizards Book**
$9.95, 1-58062-396-4

Everything® is a registered trademark of Adams Media Corporation.

For more information, or to order, call 800-872-5627 or visit everything.com
Adams Media Corporation, 260 Center Street, Holbrook, MA 02343

We Have

EVERYTHING KIDS'®!

Everything® Kids' Baseball Book
$9.95, 1-58062-489-8

Everything® Kids' Joke Book
$9.95, 1-58062-495-2

Everything® Kids' Money Book
$9.95, 1-58062-322-0

Everything® Kids' Nature Book
$9.95, 1-58062-321-2

Everything® Kids' Online Book
$9.95, 1-58062-394-8

Everything® Kids' Puzzle Book
$9.95, 1-58062-323-9

Everything® Kids' Space Book
$9.95, 1-58062-395-6

Everything® Kids' Witches and Wizards Book
$9.95, 1-58062-396-4

Available wherever books are sold!

For more information, or to order,
call 800-872-5627 or visit everything.com

Adams Media Corporation, 260 Center Street, Holbrook, MA 02343

Everything® is a registered trademark of Adams Media Corporation.